CHRISTIANITY IN
THE ROMAN EMPIRE

CHRISTIANITY IN
THE ROMAN EMPIRE

BY

HAROLD MATTINGLY,
HON. LITT.D. (N.Z.) , M.A. (CANTAB.) , F.B.A., F.S.A.

W · W · NORTON & COMPANY · INC · NEW YORK

These Lectures were delivered as a course of Open Lectures, arranged by the Faculty of Arts, to Staff and Students of the University of Otago in March and April, 1954.

Published simultaneously in Canada by
George J. McLeod Limited
Toronto

PRINTED IN THE UNITED STATES OF AMERICA

1 2 3 4 5 6 7 8 9 0

CONTENTS

CHAPTER 1

THE ROMAN EMPIRE

For the subject of these lectures I am indebted to my friend Professor Manton. But, while thanking him, I like to think that I might unaided have made the same choice. For the theme is in a remarkable way suited to tie together past and present. The roots of the tree are set deep in the classical past; we still take our repose under the shade of its boughs. The past is well worthy of study for its own interest and beauty, but we study it today for our own sakes as well—because it still works on in our world, still has lessons to teach us—and because it is just human not to live only in one dimension of time—the absorbing present—but also by memory in the past and by hope and aspiration in the future.

All the great religions of the world speak to the passing generations of that which is outside the time order, the Eternal, that ' which was in the beginning, is now and ever shall be.' Some of these religions—not all—are very closely related to history. Mohammed, great prophet of Islam, rose to sudden greatness at the very moment in the seventh century when the Empires of Rome and Persia had fought one another to a standstill. Jesus Christ, the Eternal Word, ' who was in the beginning with God ', was born in the Palestine of Herod the Great and, as we repeat in the Creed, ' suffered under Pontius Pilate '. The sacred history of Mithras, on the other hand—his birth from the rock, his solemn meal with the Sun-god, his slaying of the great bull— is quite outside time. The early history of Christianity cannot be fully understood without a knowledge of the world into which it came. The early Church soon became aware of a natural harmony between the ' tremendous majesty of the Augustan peace ' and the coming of the Prince of Peace Himself. Roman Virgil in his fourth

5

Eclogue had told of the birth of a wonderful child with whom was to end the age of sin and sorrow and the Age of Gold return. It was easy to see a fulfilment of the prophecy in the Babe of Bethlehem. Milton, in his *Ode on the Nativity,* has given noble expression to a similar thought in the passage beginning, ' No war or battle's sound, Was heard the world around'. There is always an element of falseness in these large comparisons. The parallels are not as exact as they seem. But the fact remains—there *is* a remarkable similarity between the rise of the world Empire and the rise of the religion destined to world rule. There are general truths—as broad as barn doors—which may be overlooked, just because it is impossible not to see them.

I need waste no long time on explaining the general plan of these lectures. We shall be covering a great extent both of time and space. We shall be glancing in passing at quite a lot of history: I will try to keep my story simple and help you with an occasional date or reference. All one can hope to do is to draw a few vivid pictures, with the main strokes correct. It is unfortunately not possible to illustrate these lectures as fully with materials of various kinds as I should like. But, as we are so fortunate as to have ideal conditions for Magic Lantern projection, I can show you, now and, then, a few slides of Roman coins—an invaluable source of information for many sides of ancient life, religion included. In the maze of historical events we shall try to see forms, patterns that can mean something to us. We risk, of course, seeing what is not there. But this is what the Greeks called a καλὸς κίνδυνος, a beautiful risk. If any of you care to read for yourselves on these subjects, I will try to supply a list of some suitable books. You all know something of the first term of my subject, Christianity: the second term, ' the Roman Empire ', will not be so familiar. That is why I am devoting this first lecture to it—that you may realize something of the environment into which the Church was born, with which it had long to struggle,—in which it was, finally, to rule.

One pattern was recognized of old in the ancient world— that of the great Empires—Babylon, Assyria, Egypt, Persia, the Greek of Alexander the Great and, finally, the Roman —each with its wealth of civilization and religion, lending unity and purpose to the masses of individual races and cities. Greece, with her marvellous flowering of individual genius, added something new of incalculable value. But Greek genius fell short on the practical side. Greece could never create a stable system in which her civilization could grow and thrive. The vast Empire of Alexander began to crumble as soon as he was dead. To Rome in due course fell the succession. Rome created a world order that would stand. Greece conquered her conqueror (*Graecia capta ferum victorem cepit*) and, through the Roman Empire, the Greek inheritance has descended to us. Lovers of Greece, who find it hard to forgive Rome for her injuries to Greece in the last two centuries before Christ, should not forget the amends that were made afterwards.

How did the Roman Empire come to be? In the Western Mediterranean, which Alexander did not live long enough to conquer—could he have conquered it if he had?—one city state gradually rose to supremacy in the Italian peninsula. She fought a series of desperate wars with the great Phoenician state of Carthage, trembled on the brink of defeat and finally emerged victorious. Now came progress beyond Italy—the spread of Roman civilization, assisted by Roman arms, over the barbarian peoples of the West—the clash in the East with the Successor kingdoms after Alexander, Macedon, Syria, Egypt—and the slow but sure spread of Roman influence, partly by armed force, partly by diplomacy, but also by the attraction for many states of the stable order which Rome, and only Rome, seemed to offer. In the last century before our era the Fortune of Rome —her peculiar destiny—was manifest. She was the power marked out by native capacity, geographical position and conjunction of events to give unity to a distracted world. For one long moment she wavered. The burden seemed almost too great; Rome, invincible without, seemed like to crash from within. But, after strange vicissitudes and desperate perils, the goal was reached and Rome found a new government, capable of ruling an Empire. The divine plan

—some would call it the sport of capricious fortune—was realized. An age was rising in which unity, not diversity, was to be the key note.

What was this Rome that now proposed to rule the world? The constitution of the Roman Republic was generally regarded as a mixed one—with the claims of the rich, the noble and the masses nicely balanced. In fact, it was the senate, an oligarchy of rank and landed wealth, that held control. It won this position by its firm traditions and by sheer ability. It limited the powers of the theoretically supreme people and kept a firm hand on the ambitions of the individual senator. It was this ' assembly of kings ' that founded Roman greatness. But, as Rome's power extended overseas, the provincial governors—and the armies under them—became unmanageable; for the armies began to look to their general, not to the senate, for their rewards. The Republic ended in a struggle between rival generals—the senate striving in vain to maintain its own position between them. Julius Cæsar, triumphing over his great rival, Pompey, found himself in 45 B.C. supreme; everyone looked to him to say what came next.

But the final solution was not yet. Rome was a state that ' could not endure either complete freedom or complete slavery '. Julius fell a victim to the daggers of Brutus and Cassius on the famous Ides of March, 44 B.C., because he would not respect the deep distaste of Rome for kingship. The murder could not revive the dying Republic; it *did* mean that no autocrat was yet to rule by the Tiber. Octavian, heir and adopted son of Julius, emerging victorious from the complicated struggles that followed the murder, in the last act defeating Mark Antony and Cleopatra in 31 B.C., found a way to graft the new office of ' Emperor ' on to the old Roman constitution. To the subjects of the Empire the Emperor was only not a king, because he was something more, a ' king of kings'. But in Rome real power was veiled by constitutional forms. As commander-in-chief of the armies the Emperor was ' imperator ', an old name with a new meaning. As representative of the Roman people he held the tribunician power—

sacrosanct, able to veto any action in the state that might imperil the people's interests, able to protect the individual citizen. He was *pontifex maximus,* head of Roman religion. Other special powers were added—often unsought for, just because he seemed to be the only one who could wield them. His *auctoritas*—influence, reputation—was immense and unrivalled. As the greatest of all patrons he could address the mass of citizens as his clients; the relation of patron and client, we must remember, was one of close love and trust. He could speak even more intimately as a father to his children. The Roman State was still described as *senatus populusque Romanus,* the senate and people of Rome. The senate had honour in plenty and a fair array of duties; it was also the chosen partner of the Emperor. Through divisions within and lack of initiative and courage it soon sank to be a mere tool. Yet individual senators were indispensable for the higher posts in the Emperor's service. The knights, the second order of the Roman nobility, supplied the Emperor with assistants of trained business ability; subordinate officers were drawn from the freedmen and slaves. The Roman people lost their political powers down almost to the last fraction. But they had their consolations— the bread and circus races, Juvenal's *panem et circenses;* for the Emperor, looking on them as his central constituency, chose to keep them in good humour by feeding and pampering them. They were spoilt children—sometimes, like spoilt children, very naughty indeed.

Such then was the Roman Empire at its centre—a continuation of the Republic, with a new supreme magistrate, equipped with a vast array of powers—all this, ' because peace demanded the concentration of power in one hand '. This magistrate is the Cæsar of the New Testament, whose edict goes out that ' all the world shall be enrolled ', whose image and superscription stand on the tribute money, of whom the Jews declare ' that they have no king but Cæsar '. This Cæsar was such a ruler as the world had never yet seen, virtually as absolute as any Great King of the East, but ruling a much larger realm, and ruling it with a much greater average of virtue and wisdom. But there were two important qualifications of this autocracy. There was always an element of uncertainty about the succession. No one principle—hereditary, adoptive, elective—was ever firmly established. Though the Empire might look eternal, no one dynasty could claim to be—or, shall we say? make good the claim. The other qualification was this: the Empire, once accepted as a necessity, gathered round it an ever increasing civil and military service. It was inevitable that the system should come to tyrannize over each Emperor of the moment, that caprice, never to be completely excluded, mattered less and less, that the Emperor should end by being as much the prisoner of his office as the meanest serf among his subjects.

The Emperor of the early Empire was the 'princeps', the first man in the state, chosen and maintained because of his merits. The later Emperor was a master—almost a god—the object of tremendous awe, withdrawn from all vulgar contacts. The change may have been inevitable—that the Emperor should come to be to his Romans what he was from the first to the mass of his subjects. But the change was accelerated by the military anarchy of the third century, when Emperor after Emperor fell victim to the swords of officers or men. To secure some immunity for the Emperor Diocletian (A.D. 283-305) surrounded him with the awe and ceremony of a Great King.

How are we to form a conception of the world that was organized within the Roman Empire? First of all it was vast in extent. Except for the Parthian kingdom in the Middle East, it included the whole civilized world around the Mediterranean. Distant China lay apart in its separate world. All the great cultures of antiquity were contained within it—Babylonian, Egyptian, Hittite, Phoenician, Etruscan, Greek. Around its edges lay the barbarian peoples—destined perhaps some day to be civilized under Roman influence. The population cannot be guessed at all closely. Imperial Rome may have numbered something like a million souls in all. The total population of the Empire might be estimated as of the order of eighty millions, with a wide margin of uncertainty up or down. Some provinces, like Asia, with many cities, were populous. In others, with pasture and mountains, the numbers will have been relatively very small.

The Empire has two aspects, one of unity, the other of diversity. Unity meant, at first, little more than a common subjection to one paramount authority. The subjects of the Empire were united in obedience to the laws, in payment of the taxes of Cæsar. Imperial citizenship—that is to say, Roman citizenship—belonged at first only to Rome, Italy and a strictly limited range of specially favoured communities and individuals. But, as time went on, the imperial stamp was more widely impressed. Roman citizenship spread, until, early in the third century, A.D. 212-213, Caracalla extended it to the mass of subjects everywhere. The old principle—that no man could belong at the same time to two cities—was virtually abrogated. St. Paul had the imperial citizenship; as Roman citizen he could claim exemption from being beaten with rods, could appeal to Cæsar at Rome. But he was also a citizen of Tarsus, 'no mean city', and proud to be. In the later Empire the peoples of Gaul, Africa, Illyricum, who had nothing Roman in their origins, counted themselves full heirs of the Roman patrimony and would boast of descent from the twins suckled by the she-wolf.

Within this unity diversity, of course, of various kinds persisted. The backward peoples, as they unlearned their fierce nationalism, put off with it much of their native tradition; they exchanged it—much to their advantage— for one richer and more varied. But, even so, much of the old pattern of life long survived—scattered dwellings of Britons and Germans, nomadic life for the tribes of the interior of Africa and the sheiks of the Arabian desert. But the old civilizations within the Empire resisted dissolution; if they took something from the new order, they contributed generously to it. Antioch and Alexandria, the two great capitals of the East, maintained a rude independence against which more than one Emperor beat in vain. Strong above all was the influence of Greece. Political power was lost for ever, but in art, literature, philosophy, Greece still ruled. The civilization of the Empire was as much Greek as Roman. The success of the Empire, as far as it was realized, was achieved by the alliance of the political sagacity and practical ability of the Roman with the immense resources of the Greek mind. Other influences might contest the field with the Greek here and there—for instance, the old influence of Babylonian astrology—but, on the whole, none could seriously challenge its supremacy.

The Roman Empire was essentially a vast confederacy of cities. It was in the city—and in the city of the Greek and Roman pattern—that civilization centred. It was in the city that men could still enjoy that modicum of self-government that was allowed them; it was in the city that the social pleasures—shows, banquets, baths—were to be enjoyed. The country districts were either ancillary to cities or, where divorced from them, backward and unprosperous. In the cities ran all the fresh interest, all the novelty of life. It was the backwoods countrymen, the *pagani,* who still clung to the old ways, who became the ' pagans ' when the cities were all open to the influence of Christianity. Even in the cities the pressure of the central government severely limited any real independence. But there was still opportunity for rich men to deserve the gratitude of their fellow-townsmen by munificent gifts and to reap their reward in the shape of showy, if unsubstantial, honours. In the late Empire this not unattractive picture was marred by financial stress. The burden of collecting the taxes was laid on the city nobility, the senates, and this led to a desperate flight from office.

The Augustan peace brought with it a new ease of travel and new opportunities for trade. But there was no Free Trade in the Empire. It was divided into a number of customs districts and the government took its toll of indirect taxes. Many an enterprising individual made his fortune, but no great commercial class emerged. The government thwarted any such development, partly by its shortsighted economic policies, partly by confiscation of great fortunes. In the late Empire many state factories competed with and ousted private enterprises. Taxation, by the bye, seems to have been moderate at first. The late Empire—like some modern states—cost too much to run; when an emergency like barbarian invasion was added, the mills of taxation ground exceedingly small. Economic disorder and misery—they are a main symptom, if not cause, of the Decline and Fall of Rome.

Nationalism was on the decline. The old passionate loyalties were gradually being forgotten. Even the dominant Greco-Roman strain would come to be diluted to the point where it lost its special quality. There was much inter-marriage of peoples of different races. Nationality, if still felt as a principle of division, was so more in a cultural than in a strictly national sense. Society was organized in a series of castes. At the top, the Roman nobility, senate and knights, then the Roman people, the freedmen, the slaves, the local senators, then the masses of the subject peoples. Slavery was still recognized as a normal condition, but passage by enfranchisement into the body of free citizens went steadily forward. We meet in the New Testament the challenge of the idea of brotherly love to the whole institution of slavery, but there is no immediate movement for wholesale enfranchisement. Actually, slavery was on the decline, partly because there was a less constant supply of fresh slaves, partly because slavery was a poor system economically. Yet for a long time the very poor might be reduced to selling their unwanted daughters into slavery. The movement of the late Empire was towards serfdom, not slavery—the fettering of the labourer to his sod or to his inherited profession.

And now for a glance at the machinery by which this vast Empire was run. The Empire was divided into a number of administrative districts or provinces. Those in which armies had to be maintained were, almost without exception, governed for the Emperor by his legates, of the rank of praetor or consul; a few minor provinces had knights only in command, procurators; one of these was Pontius Pilate. The older and more peaceful provinces were governed by the senate, who sent out to them men with the status of consul or praetor—*pro consule, pro praetore*. On the edges were a number of client kingdoms, which tended to be merged in provinces. Of these was the Galilee of Herod Antipas of the Gospels. The governor was, of course, something like a little king during his term of office; but the Emperors had no use for petty tyrants and usually managed to avenge, if not to prevent, abuses. Rome made herself responsible for public order, general finance and the administration of the larger scale justice; but she began by employing very moderate staffs and left a great deal to be dealt with locally. The cities, however, ran into serious financial troubles and the Emperors were led on to interfere by appointing special supervisors. But it was the fourth century only that saw a vast inflation of the Civil Service—which seems to have pleased the Romans as little as a newer inflation does many of us today.

In relation to the vast task of imperial defence the Roman army was very small. It consisted of less than half a million men, legionaries and auxiliaries, in approximately equal numbers. These armies were mainly strung along the frontiers of the border provinces, along Rhine, Danube and Euphrates. In the peaceful provinces soldiers would only rarely be seen and in small numbers. The Emperor had his household troops in Rome—the praetorian guard in particular; but there was no field army, ready to be turned to any quarter where trouble threatened. In case of emergency troops had to be transferred from one frontier to another. There was grave disadvantage here, not mitigated until Diocletian (A.D. 283). But for a long time the Emperors were too much afraid of possible rivals; a field army would be a standing temptation to ambitious soldiers. It is easy to argue—it is probably true—that this army was not large enough for the Empire. But military service had lost its attraction for many of the subjects; conscription, always possible in theory, was not used except in real emergencies. The result was that the Empire usually stood on the defensive, resolutely guarding its own, but seldom extending its bounds. Later, when the assault of barbarian tides on the frontiers became almost incessant, this theory of fixed lines of defence, this ' Maginot line ' theory, revealed all its weaknesses. There were no fundamental improvements in arms or tactics that might have made up the deficiency. The art of war was now being developed more among barbarians than in the Empire. The most effective new arms—especially the heavy knights, the 'cataphractarii'—were borrowed from Sarmatians or Persians. The generals of the fourth century were commonly of German or Gothic birth.

We have been on a tour of the Empire at large. Let us end by looking rather more closely at the corner of the world in which Christianity was born. The Jews had returned from exile under Persian protection to found their little religious kingdom. To Jerusalem as their spiritual centre the numerous Jews of the Diaspora looked. In the second century B.C. the Seleucid kings of Syria, successors of the Persians, tried to impose Greek civilization on the Jews. The successful resistance of the Maccabees led to a new state, ruled by kings who were also High Priests. By the beginning of our era the kingdom had passed to an able, unscrupulous Edomite, Herod the Great, while lesser princes ruled little principalities nearby. Luke's Lysanias, tetrarch of Abilene, is one of these. Soon after the death of Herod, Judaea was made a province under a procurator from Rome; among these governors came in due course Pontius Pilate. In Galilee the tetrarch Herod still ruled—often at variance with the Roman governor. Well to the north lay the great province of Syria, with its army; its governor had a general right of supervision over the little districts south, Judaea included.

Unlike most of the peoples of the Empire the Jews could not forget their lost independence. In spite of all Roman toleration for their religion, they hated Rome and dreamed of a Messiah who should set them free. But there were divisions among them. The Sadducees, calculating time-servers, reckoned on working in collaboration with the Roman government. The Pharisees concentrated their attention on the keeping of the Law; from politics they professed to keep aloof. But the Zealots maintained armed resistance and hoped for nothing less than a complete deliverance from Rome. One of the disciples of Jesus was a Zealot and many people will certainly have credited Him with leanings in the same direction. Jesus might teach again and again that His kingdom was not of this world, but it was very hard to turn the mind of the Jews towards the new Messianic hope. It was as a rebel against Rome that the Jews delivered up Jesus to Pilate, as a rebel that Pilate sent Him to be crucified. We learn from the Gospels that Pilate was quite aware that a wrong was being done, but that he was accustomed to work together with the High Priest and his Sadducees and lacked the courage to resist, when he heard that his own loyalty to Cæsar might be called in question.

We have taken a very brief survey of the Empire in its main outlines. It would be very interesting—but also very difficult—to survey in a like way its spiritual outlook. It was essentially conservative, against sudden change. Its values were noble birth, and wealth, especially landed wealth—less material advantages with most people ranking second. Unity tended to predominate over diversity. If you looked back to the past, you had your vision of the ancient Age of Gold; you could fancy to yourself that it was now restored. The great models of the past—in war, politics, art, literature—remained unrivalled; you did not expect them to be surpassed. At its best the Empire could be seen as the *optimus status rerum,* the best state that could be realized. If you looked to the future, the chief prospect was the eternal duration of Rome and her Empire. Even for the Christians the Empire seemed to stand between the world and the terrors of the last times. For the Stoics the Empire would endure until the whole world was dissolved in fire. One main aspect of the thought of the Empire—its religions and philosophies—will form the subject of the next lecture.

CHAPTER 2

THE RELIGIONS OF THE ROMAN EMPIRE

If one spoke of the 'religion' of the Empire in the singular, there would be a distinct suggestion of the untrue; the Empire had many religions—not very well co-ordinated. But, in spite of that, most of these religions had enough features in common to enable us to consider them under one head.

In the centre stands the polytheism of Greece and Rome —the twelve great Olympian deities, with numerous others of subordinate rank below them. Zeus and Jupiter, Hera and Juno, Athena and Minerva—the equations had all been worked out. There was virtually one system for the two countries. But Greece contributed much more than half the wealth of mythology, of matter for literary and artistic illustration. The great gods were closely related to the order of nature and the destinies of nations; but there were minor powers to care for the house and hearth, for the details of individual life, for a man's happiness and security. The whole world is alive—spiritual reality behind everything that we see and touch. Next to the Greco-Roman come the great worships of Egypt and Asia Minor. The animal gods of Egypt remained a peculiarity—object of amusement or repulsion. But the mother-goddess, Isis, and her majestic consort, Serapis, enjoyed worship far beyond the land of the Nile. At its best there was purity and tenderness, dignity with simplicity in the worship of the great Mother; some thought of her as the 'Panthea', the one reality behind the many names. Another Great Mother was the Cybele of Phrygia, adopted by Rome before 200 B.C. and, under the Empire, travelling far to all lands. Hers was a wild emotional cult, ill matched with Roman *gravitas;* but its processions,

17

its solemn washing of the divine image, its bath of bull's blood as a cleansing from evil—all made it vastly popular. Mithras, the Persian god of light, came to Rome through Cilician pirates in the last century B.C. His cult spread wide, especially through the army. The city states had still their old gods. Some of these attained a wider importance— Jupiter Dolichenus, Elagabalus of Emesa, Diana of Ephesus, Atargatis, the ' Syrian goddess '. Ancient Hittite deities survived in Anatolia, Phoenician Baals and Ashtoreth in the Phoenician homeland and in Carthage; the *Dea Caelestis* had a great vogue under the Empire. When we come to the backward, the barbarian peoples we find a welter of gods and goddesses with uncouth native names, but now commonly equated to Greek and Roman gods. You have only to turn the pages of Dessau's *Select Latin Inscriptions* to meet them by the hundred. These ancient deities passed through an *interpretatio Graeca* or *Latina* and emerged as equivalents of the great classical gods. In their worship quaint and savage elements will often have survived for a very long time. Rome occasionally seems to have broken her general rule of tolerance when faced with such an ugly thing as human sacrifice; it seems to have been for this more than for dangerous nationalism that she suppressed the Druids in Gaul and Britain.

It is a motley picture that appears, but it has features that come again and again. There is a spiritual side to everything material, everything human; there are gods of the heaven, earth and elements, gods of the city and the home, nymphs of rivers and trees, gods who preside over human hearts and destinies. These powers are conceived in human shape, exempt from human sufferings, but capable of human emotions. The supreme god—usually recognized in theory—is not always prominent. The emphasis is on the many, on polytheism, in fact. The many gods are like satraps or governors of provinces in the Empire of the Great King.

The theory is vague but inclusive and tends to promote religious tolerance. πολλαὶ μορφαὶ τῶν δαιμονίων—' There are many shapes of things spiritual', wrote the Greek tragedian,

Euripides.) As long as experience grows, your knowledge of those shapes may grow with it. If you find a people worshipping a god of unknown name, there is no cause for surprise or vexation. A little inquiry may lead you to realize that this is only a new form of Jupiter or Apollo or, perhaps, two or more familiar powers rolled into one. The mixing of attributes of several gods—syncretism—is often to be observed. All the gods were expressions of spiritual reality somewhere far from us; what need for surprise if there may be larger unities, comprising what we see as separate—if all the goddesses, for instance, may be so many shapes of the one goddess, Isis?

This world of many gods, in human form, is far too large to classify under names, but can be presented in some sort of reasonable order—by provinces. There are the great gods of the material universe, often associated as patrons and protectors with particular cities; close on them follow a host of similar powers, only of lower rank. There are the Fortunes, Τύχαι, Genii, of persons and places. There are the spirits of human emotions and aspirations—*Felicitas, Pax, Salus, Spes* and the rest. And—a particularly Roman conception—there are little deities connected with particular acts—with all the stages of human life—suckling, crawling, walking—with all the phases of agricultural labour—harrowing, ploughing, felling and burning trees.

Our modern world has come a very long way from this world of polytheism, its gods and goddesses, its immortal men and women. But can we be sure that our modern view is really right, that we have done much more than change our metaphors? If Δῖνος βασιλεύει τὸν Δί᾽ ἐξεληλακώς—'if Jet is king for he has thrown out Jove'—are we much nearer truth? Polytheism supplied a conception of the world, admirably suited to art and poetry, and useful as a form of thought even to those who had no real belief in it. The pagan deities were felt as powers even by the Christians who denied their divinity; they were generally regarded as δαίμονες, intermediate between gods and men and deluding men into paying them divine worship. The Christian who risked his life by refusing to sacrifice to Venus or Apollo

19

knew very well that he was up against some force. We might prefer to call it 'crowd emotion' or something of that kind, depersonalizing it. But I am not sure that we do not carry this 'depersonalizing' too far. If we wish to interpret the world at all, we have to import into it something out of our own minds. Whatever the footstep that we find in the sand it is liable to turn out to be our own. In Europe under Hitler there were certainly δαίμονες at work; and, whatever they may have been in themselves, they seemed to have the power of obsessing human beings. Polytheism is a stage through which the race has passed and in our subconscious mind the effects of it are still powerful.

A little now about the forms of pagan worship. The god or goddess conceived as man or woman,—only of power and beauty more than human and immune from death—would be represented by the image, the idol, of gold, silver, or stone—the symbol of the divine power, not itself. The absurdity of 'bowing down to wood or stone' was palpable even to the pagan. But undoubtedly some special charm or potency was felt to cling to the idol.

The god has his house, his temple to dwell in and his altar at which to receive sacrifice. Sacrifice—either unbloody, wine and incense, or bloody, flesh of oxen, sheep and goats —could be thought of as a symbol of spiritual homage. But the bloody sacrifice carried too clearly the suggestion that the gods, like men, need flesh to nourish them. The common form of prayer was the vow, *votum*. The worshipper, making his request, promises a sacrifice in requital and, in due course, pays it. It is a strictly business-like proposition; *do ut des,* 'I give that you may give too.' Special services of prayer would be held on occasions of special need; the attributes of the gods would be set out on gorgeously arrayed couches. There would be the domestic worship of the spirits of the hearth and home, sacrifices in the country to protect the crops and herds. Paganism looked more to the community than to the individual; but the vow could give expression to individual hopes; and even the great Olympians could be the objects of individual piety. The great Scipio, the conqueror of Carthage, used to spend hours in the temple of Jupiter on the Capitol in communion with the god. There was one special development of paganism in which the hopes and fears of the individual really came into their own—what we call the ' mystery religions '. In them the believer claimed to come into touch with a divine helper and friend and, by mystic participation in his life, to receive the hope of a blessed immortality. The vocabulary of St. Paul includes the word ' mystery ' and proves that he was familiar with this side of ancient religion. As initiation was required for admission to the mysteries, and the secret was well kept, we have only an approximate idea of even such a famous cult as that of Demeter and Kore, the divine mother and her daughter, at Eleusis. The initiate entered into the experience of the search of the sorrowing mother for her lost Persephone, and human immortality was shadowed forth under the symbol of the new-born grain.

Some students of the ancient world find very unkind things to say about these religions and their devotees. They adopt the current view of many pagans—a man should be content to be submerged under the vast movements of States and should find his consolation, if consolation he must have, in the hope of posthumous fame. The craving for assistance from above, the desire for life after the grave are ' the deeply base wishes of the socially unprivileged'. This is very severe and very unjust. As long as there are people to whom life does not immediately offer full satisfaction, are we to deny them any compensation? Is the individual so worthless? What is a State if it is only composed of many ciphers? There is always something unreal about this excessive devaluation of the individual. Even its preachers cannot practise it themselves.

Immortality is a vital point in personal religion. Life after death supplies the simplest answer to the failures and frustrations of life. If the soul, as Plato says, is immortal and is capable of sounding the heights and depths of good and evil, human destiny may be terrible, but it is never despicable. Paganism had no clear answer here. It was mainly concerned with the things that go on from generation to generation, the natural order, the State—not with the individuals who come and go; even when immortality was promised, as by the mysteries, it was rather as a special and conditional boon than as the natural destiny of all. Grave inscriptions from the Empire survive in their tens of thousands to give us some idea of popular belief. Some are definitely negative: ' I was, I am not, I don't care.' Often forms of symbolism are used in ornament which suggest survival of death—the ascent to the sky, the voyage to the isles of the blest, the victory in battle. What is most remarkable is the very general care taken to secure a worthy monument where a man's bones may rest in peace with his friends. There is something deeper than reflective belief here—an insistence on retaining some part in the world that one has known. The practice of inhumation, which was growing at the expense of cremation, has some connection with belief in survival. If the body is reduced to ashes, all that seems possible for the soul is a vague, shadowy existence, very far from that of the quick, the solid body. But the body, committed to earth the mother, may be thought of as the seed which is sown to decay, but to be reborn.

Astrology was not exactly a religion or a science either, though it claimed to be. Yet it had a very large following, even in the higher orders of society, who often claimed to be religiously emancipated. Its influence was evil. It led to many a political plot, many an execution. It bound the individual in a web of destiny, inexorable, ineluctable. The ' world rulers of this darkness ', of whom St. Paul speaks, may have been the rulers of the planets, conceived of as inimical to the soul as it leaves the earth. Magic flourished in holes and corners. You might invoke its aid to foreknow the future, to win love, to ruin your enemies. It dwelt in the very slums of religion; its powers would be not so much the great gods as an infinity of mischievous δαίμονες or demons, ready to plague mankind.

Paganism was inclined to be tolerant because it was essentially inclusive. Where there were already so many gods, what harm can there be in a few more? We shall see later how tolerance broke down in practice, not for any reason of creed but for two practical reasons—the fear the authorities felt of a menace to the public order—the exasperation of the mob against nonconformists who seemed to bring down on men the wrath of heaven.

Pagan thought was repulsive to many men, because of its lack of seriousness, its vagueness and its flippancy. It might pass as suitable for art and literature, but as a serious explanation of the nature of things—no. The philosophers could see that clearly enough; but they were seldom anxious to carry their challenge far. Pagan morality was a more serious trouble. When grossly immoral practices were attributed to the divine powers, how expect too much from men? Any lover of antiquity will raise some protest against St. Paul's sweeping denunciations in *Romans*. The Greeks and Romans were not universally debased; they had deep regard for many values, many virtues. That Christianity at once demanded higher standards, particularly in sexual morality, it would be ridiculous to deny. It is of course even sillier to paint fancy pictures of the joy of life, the lost joy, in the pagan world. It was a hard world for the under-dog. But the fault of paganism lay not only in its thought or its morality. It took little account of the two tremendous ideas of the love of God for man and the love of man for his fellows; they were in the world—but it needed Christianity to make them come alive for the many. Conversion, as Professor Nock has pointed out, might often be a gentle, gradual process; but the distance between the shores—the shore that you left and the further shore to which you crossed—seen after the crossing was immense.

Philosophy demands to understand, where religion may be content to experience. A man may follow both; he may worship with his fellows, and yet as a philosopher seek for explanations that they can dispense with. In antiquity, philosophy was one of Greece's greatest gifts to the world. By the time of the Empire the schools of Plato and Aristotle had declined from their heights; the vitality of philosophy was to be found rather in the moral philosophies that came in from the fourth century B.C.—the Cynics, the Stoics and the Epicureans. The Cynics, at their best not ignoble preachers of the simple life, carried simplicity and truth to nature to shamelessness and independence to impertinence. Far more important were the Stoics, who soon found themselves very much at home in Rome. They believed in a fiery soul of the Universe, from which we all come, to which we all return. Their glory was in their moral teaching—the self-sufficiency of the sage, the good man, the supreme value of virtue, the relative indifference of everything else. Perhaps Stoicism rose as high as human nature, unassisted, can rise. Its great blemish was its spiritual pride; it forgot to make due allowance for man's dependence on God. Its virtues appealed strongly to the best of the Romans; Marcus Aurelius, a bright star among the good Emperors, was a Stoic. As a rule the Stoics were not unfriendly to popular religion. They admitted it as a necessity for the masses who could not live on the heights of philosophy. The crude myths could be regarded as allegorical explanations of natural phenomena or of moral truths. The Stoics, in fact, found ways to share the general tolerance of paganism. A Stoic might be willing to be martyred for his moral convictions—not for publicly defying common religious beliefs; those are right enough—for the people.

Very different were the followers of the gentle Epicurus. Like the Stoics they sought the supreme good in the soul of the individual; unlike them, they sought it in pleasure, in happiness, not in virtue; virtue for the sake of happiness, not for its own sake. They were not the grovellers after pleasure that their enemies represented them to be. The best of them tried to live lives void of offence, gladdened in particular by the love of friends. They saw the chief enemy to peace of mind in religion—in the fear of the gods, the fear of what might come after death. These made happiness impossible; therefore these must go. There are no gods in the vulgar sense; there is no life after death, for the soul, like everything else, is a chance formation of soulless atoms. Once rid of extravagant hopes and fears man may pluck such happiness as the limitations of life allow. The Epicureans were commonly stigmatized as atheists, and the stigma was earned if by gods we mean the busybody gods of common belief. But Epicurus had his own gods, beings of superhuman beauty and grace, dwelling in space between the worlds, completely happy—and, therefore, certainly not touched by human miseries. Images of joy and peace can come from these radiant beings and communicate something of their essence to men. This philosophy, though celebrated by one Roman poet of genius, Lucretius, was not vigorous or practical enough to appeal much to Romans. By the Empire it had passed its height of influence; but Walter Pater, in his *Marius the Epicurean*, may be right in suggesting that many followers of this gentle philosophy found a new spiritual home in Christianity. The Epicureans belonged to the small minority that refused to accept the whole basis of ancient religion. Of course, like all extreme materialists, they destroyed their own beliefs with those of others; for if the mind is only a chance and temporary collection of atoms, what reason to expect truth from its findings?

There was a wonderful revival of Platonism in the third century, centring round the giant figure of Plotinus. There is true sublimity in his thought of the union of the soul with ultimate truth—a Beatific Vision that might be vouchsafed a few times in a lifetime. His followers—usually called Neo-Pythagoreans, in succession to the Neo-Platonists—declined to a lower level of thought, in which theurgy, the production of marvels through the conjuration of divine powers, played a large part. Both these philosophies, unlike the Epicurean, accepted the popular paganism, while giving it their own esoteric meanings. Julian the Apostate, who attempted to check Christianity and substitute for it a refined and clarified form of paganism, worked hand in glove with the Neo-Pythagoreans of his time. There was colour, there was adventure in these late phases of Greek philosophy, but no real independence of the errors of the vulgar. The philosophies even came out as defenders of paganism.

The Jews were a religious anomaly in the Empire. Originally a nomad people, they had a tribal god of majesty and awe, quite unlike the Baalim and Ashtoreth, worshipped by the Canaanites ' under every green tree and on every high hill '. By a long development, strongly assisted by the great prophets, they advanced to a higher conception of God as holy as well as mighty, the God of the whole earth, not of one nation only. The Law, divinely given on Sinai, was man's guide to the good life. This exclusive religion was repugnant and unintelligible to Romans. A reading of the first chapters of Tacitus' *Histories,* Book v, leaves no doubt of this. A temple without a statue seemed ridiculous, so the fable spread that the Jews worshipped an ass's head. And this strange people, with its own ugly and unnatural ways, must condemn all other religions and mock at idols made of wood and stone. Yet the Romans found the Jews everywhere, active, able, thrusting,—a stiff-necked generation, difficult to cross. They therefore allowed them tolerance in religion even beyond the normal and let them form their separate corporations in the great Greek cities. This compromise worked reasonably well for a time; it broke down in the two great revolts under Nero and Hadrian and the Jews were finally scattered from the Holy Land. To the Roman government the Christians must for some time have been indistinguishable from the Jews; its attitude must have been largely determined by this misconception.

In a world of polytheism, unchallenged by most of the philosophies, the Jews and Christians were alike in maintaining the unity and spirituality of the divine nature. The religion of Mani—Manichaeism—which spread wide in the East in the latter part of the third century, took over and developed the old dualistic system of the Persians, with the whole world as the theatre of a mighty struggle between good and evil, at all levels, the divine, the intermediate, the human. This plausible explanation of the strife that pervades life had already appeared in some of the Gnostic sects of the second century. It is a heresy that has again and again raised its head in later Church history.

To Anatole France we owe the interesting fantasy (in *Sur la Pierre blanche),* in which Gallio, governor of Achaea, is debating with his entourage the question of a possible religion of the Empire, just when St. Paul, the missionary of the one that was actually coming, was waiting outside to be tried. That a world politically unified might naturally find religious unity too was obvious enough. But where was the impulse to unity to begin? Jupiter, the supreme god of Romans and Greeks, seems to have lacked general appeal. When Diocletian set up his new system, Jupiter, god the father, Hercules, god the son, he probably had the Christians in mind. The Sun-god of the East, worshipped in many places under different forms, came very near to being the god of the Empire; Aurelian did for a moment in A.D. 274 set him up as *dominus imperii Romani*.

In one form a religion of the Empire did arise—in the worship of the *divi*, of the good Emperors, consecrated for their merits after their death. It was a natural symbol of loyalty to the Empire; it seems to have been the form of paganism which the first persecutor general, Trajan Decius, in A.D. 249 wished to impose on his subjects at large. This worship of men as gods to us seems absurd and rather shocking. Not so to the ancients. Since the Greeks, after Alexander the Great, had accustomed themselves to the worship of living men, the theory of the romancer, Euhemerus, grew in vogue. The gods that we worship were once men on earth; they died after great achievements and, for them, have been raised to godhead. The process still goes on. *Deus est homini hominem iuvare.* ' It is divine that a man should aid his fellow-man '. To this extent even Pliny the Elder, certainly no enthusiast in religion, allows himself to follow the current view. New gods by merit are continually being produced and the good Emperors naturally take pride of place among them. The great gods had always been regarded as the protectors of the State. They do not disappear from the scene now, but they are more and more represented as the ' companions ' or ' preservers ' of the Emperors. The Emperors themselves live under constant divine protection and, on death, take their place in the imperial heaven.

This imperial religion will meet us again and again when we study the relations of Christian Church and Roman Empire. The burning of the few grains of incense to the

Genius of the Emperor was a favourite test of repentance of error and return to the ways of one's fathers. But this official religion lacked warmth and personal appeal. Perhaps this is an example of a general truth; the Empire was accepted rather than loved by the mass of its people; it did not establish its claim to deep devotion. The sentiment of devotion finds its clearest expression just when Rome was past her prime and the shadows of decline were already falling.

To sum up the results of a lecture that has ranged somewhat wide:

(1) Polytheism,—a system of many gods,—was general throughout the Empire under many forms. Its thought was very confused, its morality very imperfect. It was as a rule tolerant, not with any very lofty toleration, but with some indifference to what other people did as long as they did not attack it.

(2) There were many philosophies that denied the popular religions, philosophies that in many cases could demonstrate their weaknesses. With the one exception of the Epicureans the philosophers refused to make it their business to purify popular belief and would even contend that it was right in its own place.

(3) The Jews and Christians, as monotheists and protestors against polytheism, stood alone and sometimes together.

(4) The imperial religion, the cult of the defied Emperors, never reached its full development, never passed from official to heartfelt acceptance.

CHAPTER 3

THE CHURCH AND THE EMPIRE
DOWN TO TRAJAN

Jesus Christ 'suffered under Pontius Pilate', as one among many suspected of leading national risings against Rome. (A.D. 29?). The story in Eusebius, which he quotes from Tertullian, tells of how Tiberius received a report from Palestine about the death and resurrection of Jesus and sent it on to the senate, with indications of his approval of the new doctrine; but the senate, not having tested the matter itself, rejected the report. However, Tiberius threatened death to the accusers of the Christians. This story is generally rejected today as not being consistent with what we know in general of the early days of the Church. Tacitus, in his *Annals*, may have referred to the Crucifixion —he does occasionally refer to events of not dissimilar character in the provinces—but the passage would have stood, if at all, in the gap between Books V and VI. If Pilate reported to Tiberius, one might suppose that it would be through his superior on the spot, the governor of Syria.

We are familiar with the Christian witness about the empty tomb—also with the Jewish account, that the disciples came by night and took the body away. The ordinary Roman would shrug his shoulders; men once crucified do not rise again. The Greek—we know how the Athenians, when St. Paul spoke to them on Mars' Hill of the resurrection, at once said 'that they would hear him another day'. There is one curious piece of evidence which might have some reference, if only indirect, to the case. It is an imperial edict from Nazareth, decreeing the death penalty for tomb robbery for anyone who destroys a tomb or casts out the buried or 'with evil intent, removes them to some other spot '. Momigliano *(Claudius,* pp. 35ff., n.36) relates the edict to the quarrels between Jews and Christians under Claudius in Rome. The edict certainly seems to fit that date: before Claudius, one could not expect an imperial edict in Galilee.

The picture, as presented for example in *The Robe,* of Christianity already attracting serious attention in the reigns of Tiberius and Caligula, is probably false. Tacitus tells us how the ' awful superstition ', repressed for a time, revived and spread. Suetonius reports that Claudius expelled from Rome the Jews who were rioting at the instigation of Chrestus. The ' e ' for ' i ' in the names Christ, Christians, occurs not uncommonly; so there is hardly room to doubt that Suetonius has a confused reference to riots between Jews and Christians in Rome. Christianity, then, early reached Rome. It took root in the Emperor's own guard. The noble lady, Pomponia Graecina, wife of Plautius, the conqueror of Britain, was probably a Christian. She was accused of a foreign superstition, tried by her husband before a domestic court and acquitted.

Our knowledge of the Apostolic Age comes to us mostly from the Christian side, from the Acts of the Apostles, from the Epistles of St. Paul and other New Testament writings and, with much less certainty, from sundry Aprocryphal Gospels and Epistles. The faith of the disciples revives with the conviction that Christ is risen. Bitter persecution by the Jews fails to crush the growth of the Church. St. Paul is converted and learns of his life mission—to carry the Gospel to the Gentiles. And so the Christian Churches are one by one planted, sometimes very humble meetings in private houses. They arise in many of the cities of the East —in Jerusalem, Antioch, Ephesus, Philippi, Corinth and the rest; there are some notable exceptions, Alexandria for example. The West, apart from Rome, is hardly touched as yet. The call is to the poor and oppressed; not many wise, not many noble, not many rich are called.

It is the Jews that are the enemy. The Roman government is seen as protector, rather than persecutor. St. Paul is a friend of Sergius Paulus, governor of Cyprus. At Philippi he is scourged and imprisoned by the magistrates; but they discover their grave error—he is a Roman citizen and they had not realized it—and have to appeal to his generosity to pass it by. At Ephesus, when Demetrius the silver-smith rouses the mob against St. Paul, the town clerk tries to still the tumult with appeals to the Roman authority. In Achaea Gallio, the Roman governor, ' cares for none of these things ', when the Jews try to interest him in their quarrel with Paul. Rome is concerned with the public order, not with petty disputes on religion which no one not closely concerned in them can understand. Christians are often reminded of their duty to honour lawful authority.

The persecution of Nero fell like a thunderbolt on the Church. It seems to have lasted several years and not to have been confined to Rome. A confident tradition assigns to it the martyrdoms both of St. Peter and St. Paul. Tacitus alone in his very particular account gives the initial year, A.D. 64, and connects the persecution with the Great Fire of Rome. Suetonius *(Nero,* 16, 2) only knows of the torments inflicted on the Christians, a new, vile and pernicious superstition. We turn to the evidence of Tacitus. In A.D. 64 a large part of Rome was destroyed by a terrible fire; the Emperor, Nero, already horribly notorious as murderer of half-brother, mother and wife, was suspected of having fired his city; he had, they said, dressed up as a lyrist and sung a ' Sack of Troy ' over burning Rome. Tacitus then reports the sequel—it may be said by the way that the passage is unquestionably by Tacitus—if any part of the *Annals* is; the attempts of the old ' Higher Criticism ' to discredit the passage have failed completely:

Annals. XV. 44. . . . ' But no human effort, no generosity on the part of the Emperor, no atonement of the gods could rid Nero of the disgraceful imputation of having ordered the fire. To silence these rumours Nero found scapegoats on whom to fix the guilt and punished them with the most exquisite torments. These were the people called Christians by the mob and hated for their abominations. The originator of the name, Christus, was put to death by the procurator, Pontius Pilate, in the reign of Tiberius. For the time the horrible superstition was suppressed, but it tended to break out again, not only in

31

Judaea, the source of the mischief, but in Rome, whither all that is monstrous flows and finds a ready welcome. First to be arrested were the men who admitted the charge; then, on their information, a vast multitude were seized—not exactly on the charge of incendiarism, but of hatred of the human race. The deaths they died were aggravated by cruel mockeries. They were wrapped in the skins of wild beasts, to die under the mangling of hounds, or nailed to crosses or set to burn like torches, so that, when daylight failed, they might illuminate the night. Nero had offered his gardens for this spectacle and also gave a circus show, mingling with the crowds in the dress of a charioteer or riding in his car. All this gave birth to pity for his victims, guilty though they were and deserving of the worst possible punishments; men felt that they were being spent, not in the public interest, but to glut the cruelty of an individual.'

Tacitus, when we can check his accounts against other sources, is always—nearly always—reliable. When he connects the persecution with the Great Fire, he can be hardly mistaken. But the rest of our tradition, which extends the persecution to a wider range and knows of no special connexion with the Fire, cannot be ignored. Suetonius reports the persecution not as an atrocity, but as one of a series of salutary reforms. We shall also see, very soon, that the action of Nero as persecutor seems to have become a model for later Emperors. Tacitus, I believe, has misled us, as he often misleads, not on point of fact, but on its interpretation. The Great Fire had occurred, Nero was suspected of guilt, the Christians, with their talk of an approaching end of the age in fire, might seem very suitable scapegoats. But the examinations of the persons arrested soon took the question right away from the original occasion. The government claimed to have unearthed a sort of minor conspiracy against the human race; as we shall see, it seems to have won general approval for its action. Tacitus wants to throw mud at Nero and finds a most unfriendly interpretation of his persecution. He uses the Christians as sticks to beat Nero with. For the Christians themselves he has no real sympathy or understanding. Yet he was governor in Asia, the year after Pliny in Bithynia had raised the question of the Christians with the Emperor, Trajan; he knew, then, that Pliny had discovered that the horrible charges of crime brought against the Christians were, normally, false. No hint of this is allowed to colour his narrative here. He is guilty of telling something less than the truth. The Christians lay outside the possible range of his approval—low, unusual, no class people—it never even occurs to him that they may be right.

On what grounds were the Christians persecuted? A much disputed question—not yet certainly answered. Paganism was usually carelessly tolerant. Rome herself interfered now and then against foreign cults, but normally in the name of threatened morality. What was there in Christianity to make Rome break her general rule? Mommsen in a famous paper urged that persecution was commonly a part of police control, *coercitio*, determined not by law, but by the decision of authority from time to time that intervention was necessary to ensure public order. Another view is that the Church was persecuted as an unlicensed society. The Empire was very jealous of private societies, seeing in them sources of trouble, and therefore insisted that they should be licensed. An unlicensed club, continuing to meet after warning, would certainly expose itself to extreme penalties. Others think that the charge was High Treason, *maiestas*. It was a charge very commonly tacked on to others in the Early Empire. Or the supposed crimes of the Christians might have furnished the grounds for prosecution. Cannibalism and incest were supposed to be regular features of Church life.

None of these explanations is quite satisfactory. All may contain some element of truth. Very early, persecution ' for the name ' is certain. That is to say, to confess yourself a Christian is enough to condemn you. The principle is recognized when Pliny consults Trajan from Bithynia. It must, then, have been established by test cases, who the Christians were and how they were to be dealt with. Our evidence for events between the years A.D. 64 and A.D. 111 is so slight that we must admit that the decision against the Christians *may* have fallen within them. It seems more probable that the action of Nero against the Christians was not, in the imperial records, associated specially with the

Great Fire, or regarded as one of his more irresponsible freaks, but that it furnished a precedent for further trials and at once made persecution 'for the name' an immediate possibility for every loyal Christian. Even if the Christians were not guilty of cannibalism and incest, even if they had not fired Rome, they were, by common consent, an uncouth, uncomfortable set of killjoys, hating the normal pleasures of life and denying the people's gods. They seemed to be Jews of a kind—and yet the Jews would have none of them. The Empress Poppaea was addicted to Jewish practices; and it has been most plausibly suggested that she, to divert hatred from the Jews, used her influence with Nero to turn him against the Christians. This is only a guess—but it seems to be a reasonable one.

Close on the persecution of Nero followed the first revolt of the Jews, ending in the destruction of Jerusalem. The Church had to adapt itself to new conditions. The Empire, long seen as friend, might at any moment turn persecutor. The disastrous end of the Jewish fight with Rome might seem to mean the catastrophic end of the age of which Jesus had spoken. Perhaps the thought that the end of the world itself was not imminent may now have begun to arise. It was in this new era that our Gospels were written. The three Synoptic Gospels set out in due order for the faithful what was known and accepted of our Lord's life and ministry. They all—including St. Mark—are written under the impression of the Fall of Jerusalem, accomplished or imminent. That Jesus spoke His warnings of the coming judgement is not to be questioned; but the fresh interest in these sayings, nowhere apparent in the Acts or the Epistles of St. Paul, tells its tale. St. Luke was perhaps presenting the Christian case to sympathizers in the Greek world. St. John, of course, is years later than the Synoptics; he tells the Gospel story again with new emphasis for a new age.

The position of the Jews in the Empire was seriously changed for the worse. The didrachm, due to the Temple, had now to be paid to Jupiter of the Capitol; a special chest, the *fiscus Iudaicus,* dealt with this revenue, and became notorious for brutality and chicanery over the collection of the tax. It is most probable that, during the course of examinations to decide whether a man was a Jew and so liable to the tax, the difference between Jew and Christian became generally known as never before. Suppose a man, who is found to be circumcised and yet denies that he is a Jew. Who is he then? A Christian. Has he a special charter as the Jew has? No. Has he the right, then, to exist as a Christian? No. In this way, the original judgement of Nero against Christians may have been repeated and confirmed. There is a passage in Sulpicius Severus, a later writer thought to be copying Tacitus, about Titus holding a Council of War to decide whether or not to destroy the Temple. He himself is for destruction; the religions of the Jews and Christians will be the easier undermined. This suggests that the Jews and Christians were indeed known to be distinct, but still not clearly distinguished.

Of the second persecution, that of Domitian, late in his reign, *c*. A.D. 95, not much is known. Among the victims were Flavia Domitilla, cousin of the Emperor, banished to an island; she was certainly a Christian. Probably her husband, Flavius Clemens, put to death on this occasion, was one also; he was executed for ' atheism '; he is also described as a man *contemptissimae inertiae*—both very suitable charges against a Christian. (Suetonius, *Domitian* 15. 1.) The persecution extended to Asia. The Apocalypse is full of the sufferings of those who would not bear the mark of the Beast on their foreheads; it speaks of Pergamum ' where the seat of Satan is '. There is a clear reference to the Pergamene temple of Rome and Augustus. Persecution is clearly for refusal to worship the Emperor—the Beast. There is a curious story that Domitian, anxious to learn more of the truth, sent for the descendants of the family of the Lord from Palestine and interrogated them. When he found them to be poor, unambitious and humble people, he sent them home unharmed. Our record of this persecution is very imperfect. The Apocalypse, it seems, preserves the impression that it made—mixed, no doubt, with memories of the persecution of Nero; but we cannot read certainties out of deliberately riddling prophesies.

After the tyrant Domitian came the respectable elderly lawyer, Nerva, and, after him, the great soldier, Trajan, One famous martyrdom is known,—probably from his earlier years before he visited the East in person. The martyr was St. Ignatius, bishop of Antioch. Letters of his to sundry Churches still survive to give us a vivid impression of his faith and zeal, his fanatical devotion and his enthusiasm for his own order of bishop. An interesting story makes him appear before the tribunal of Trajan himself. Trajan inquires about his claim to be a Χριστοφόρος, to bear Christ about in his body. 'And do you not suppose,' says the Emperor, 'that I have powers in me that give me triumph over my enemies?'. Trajan is thinking of the *Victoria* and *Virtus Augusti* which are for ever appearing on the coins. The point of the story—the comparison of Christian and pagan belief—is sound; we cannot be sure that the interview ever took place.

We come now to the most interesting of all pagan *testimonia* to the early history of the Church. In A.D. 110 Trajan, seriously disquieted about the financial conditions of the cities of Bithynia, sent out as governor on a special mission his friend, the Younger Pliny. We know of Pliny as a barrister and man of letters, a great friend of Tacitus and a man of liberal and kindly character. Pliny found serious difficulties awaiting him, about many of which he consulted Trajan. Among them was the question of the Christians. Let us give Pliny himself the word:

Epistle XCVI. Pliny to the Emperor Trajan.

'It is my principle, Sir, to refer to you all points on which I am in doubt. Who better than you can guide my hesitation or buttress my ignorance? I have never attended trials of the Christians and therefore do not know what the punishment and inquiry usually are and how far they are pushed. And so I was in no slight uncertainty on several points; should any distinction of age be made or should the young be treated no otherwise than those of mature age? Should pardon be given for repentance or should a man who had once been a Christian profit nothing by ceasing to be? Should the name, if free from serious crimes, be punished or only the crimes that attach to the name? Pending your advice, the method I have followed with those who were brought before me as Christians is this. I have asked them in person whether they were Christians. If they have confessed I have repeated my inquiry a second and third time; when they persisted, I have ordered them to execution. I had no uncertainty in my mind, that whatever the character of their confession was, their persistence, their unbending obstinacy deserved extreme punishment. There were others, similarly afflicted, to whose cases, as they were Roman citizens, I added the note that they should be sent to Rome. Then, as the cases were being tried and the charges spread, as they will, more types of conduct met me. An anonymous document was produced in public, containing many names. Such of these as declared that they were not and never had been Christians I thought fit to discharge, after they, following my recital, had invoked the gods and had prayed with wine and incense before your statue, which I had ordered to be brought in with the divine figures, and had moreover cursed Christ—all acts to which it is said that those who really are Christians cannot possibly be forced. Others, named by the informer, first declared that they were Christians and subsequently denied it; they had been, but had ceased to be, some many years previously, a few as much as twenty five. All of these people adored your image and those of the gods and cursed Christ. But they kept on assuring me that the full extent of their guilt or error had been that they had been accustomed to meet on a fixed day before dawn, to sing a hymn to Christ as god and to bind themselves by an oath to be guilty of no crime, not to commit theft, robbery or adultery, not to break faith, not to deny a trust on demand; after this it had been their custom to disperse and then to meet again to take food—but ordinary food and quite innocent; they had given up doing even this after my edict, in which, following your instruction, I had forbidden clubs. All this made me feel it the more necessary to ascertain the truth from two servant-girls, whom they called deaconesses—using torture. All I could discover was an evil and extreme superstition. I therefore postponed the trial and have resorted to asking your counsel. The chief reason why I have thought it proper to consult you is the number of the persons in jeopardy. Many of all ages, of all ranks, of both sexes, are being brought into danger, and will continue to be brought. The blight of this superstition has not been confined to towns and villages; it has even spread to the country. But, in my opinion, it can be checked and cured. Certainly my statistics already show that temples, long left desolate, have begun to be thronged again, that religious ceremonies, long intermitted, are being renewed, and that there is again a market for the flesh of victims, for which till recently hardly a single buyer could be found. This all leads me to realize what a multitude of men can be reformed, if room is left for repentance.'

Epistle XCVII. Trajan, to his friend, Pliny:

' My dear Secundus, you have pursued the correct course of conduct in investigating the cases of those who were brought before you as Christians. Indeed, no general regulation can be given that would have anything like a clearcut form. They are not to be sought out; if they are denounced and proved guilty, they must be punished—providing only this, that a man who denies that he is a Christian and proves it by his act, that is to say, by praying to our gods, however suspect he may have been in the past, may now obtain forgiveness through repentance. Anonymous documents must not figure in any charge. That would be a vile precedent, not permissible in our age.'

These letters are priceless for the light that they throw on the early Church, and also on Pliny and Trajan. The Christians have for some time been prospering in Bithynia. Perhaps they had prospered even more some years back; many have ceased to be Christians, we hear. The pagan worship of the province has been suffering seriously. Now, there is a strong reaction against the Church, perhaps encouraged by the appearance of Trajan's special commissioner. Pliny himself ' has never attended the trials of Christians '. This seems to imply that such trials were now something quite familiar. Pliny is satisfied after examination that the Christians are, at any rate as a rule, innocent of horrible crimes. Yet he has no doubt that their obstinacy in itself deserves death, if persisted in. Is this really strong government—to let individuals come into fatal conflict with itself, where no clear matter of morality is involved? Pliny is not quite sure if the name in itself deserves punishment. Trajan removes this doubt. The Christian, denounced and confessing, earns death. The extreme position, ' It is forbidden to be a Christian ', is affirmed. At the same time, a noble warning is added against wanton persecution and against the hateful admission of anonymous denunciations. Trajan could be represented either as a persecutor or as a friend. As a matter of fact the knowledge that the Emperor was personally unwilling to hunt down Christians certainly acted as a deterrent on accusers, but we have only to look back to the experiences of St. Paul to see how far things have moved since his day. Then the Christian might expect protection, if not positive favour, from the Roman government. Now he must be thankful if he is permitted to escape notice. Let us sum up the development that we have been considering. The early Christians attracted little attention from the Roman government, were not persecuted, might even be protected against their enemies, the Jews. This happy state of things came to a sudden close under Nero. Tacitus has probably confused the picture by connecting the persecution too closely with the Great Fire of Rome. If the persecution had been merely one of Nero's brutal vagaries, it would not have continued to supply a precedent for Emperors after him. It is strange but true that Romans of character and position continue to speak of Christianity as a horrible superstition and have no doubt that mere persistence in it merits death. It may be as early as Nero that persecution 'for the name' began.

The revolt of the Jews must have shown up the distinction between Christians and Jews and the distinction must have been more and more clearly realized in the years following. This fact may have contributed to the persecution of Christians. They could no longer be included in the general charter that had been granted to the Jews. The question kept coming up: Is a man allowed to be a Christian? The government answer was 'No, we do not recognize such a body.'

The persecution of Domitian certainly extended from Rome to Asia; it may have been intense, but it did not last long. The Church was growing vigorously, especially in Bithynia; or is it only that our precise information is restricted to that province? We might deduce from Pliny's report that the persecution had led to a number of recantations.

Under Trajan the position was stabilized, as far as imperial policy admitted it. The Christians were still forbidden, but were not to be sought out. The Roman government is not seen quite at its best here. Its refusal to encourage persecution does it credit; not so its refusal to reconsider its general unfavourable judgment on the Church. There is some sign of an uneasy conscience in Trajan's noble reply to Pliny.

It may be noted that Christian apologists made much of the fact that only bad Emperors persecuted. This was an exaggeration of the truth. Trajan continued the practice of Nero. There was something of a moral reform at Rome, beginning with the sound old Sabine countryman, Vespasian. But the better men who now tended to rise to high positions in the State still maintained the harsh verdict on the Church.

CHAPTER 4

THE CHURCH AND THE EMPIRE: HADRIAN TO TRAJAN DECIUS AND VALERIAN

We saw in our last lecture how the revolts of the Jews led to the destruction of Jerusalem and how the wandering Jew entered on his long pilgrimage. We saw, too, how in the course of this process the difference between Christian and Jew became more and more clear to the government. The further revolts of the Jews towards the end of the reign of Trajan and the last desperate rising under Bar-Cochba, ' The Son of a Star ', sealed the fate of the race; Jerusalem became a pagan city, Aelia Capitolina.

For the whole of our long period, A.D. 117-259, the general principle of Trajan holds. The government is not anxious to stir up persecution: but it is not lawful to be a Christian. Whether persecution comes or not depends on the passions of the mob and the willingness of provincial governors to curry favour with it. Any natural disaster, famine, plague, war, may be attributed to the anger of the gods and so laid on the Christians, whose impiety has brought it down. Sometimes personal animosities will have led to attacks on individuals. Anonymous denunciations were no longer encouraged; but now and then a prosecutor will have found the courage to appear in person. The position of a Christian was always precarious; he might at any moment be faced with the alternative of suffering for his faith or denying it.

Persecution, then, was intermittent and to some extent accidental. Hadrian early in his reign was consulted by the governor of Asia about trials of Christians; he was needing advice much as Pliny had done. The reply of Hadrian only reached the next governor; it was in the tone of Trajan's reply to Pliny, insisting that mob violence and intimidation must be kept out. The Emperors of the second century were in the main men of high character, with a strong sense of imperial responsibility. But that did not save a Polycarp or Justin Martyr from suffering under Antoninus Pius or the martyrs of Lugdunum under Marcus Aurelius. The persecution at Lugdunum, c. A.D. 175-6, was peculiarly virulent and horrible. The Empire had been suffering grievously from plague and barbarian invasion and the outcry against the Christians may have been the effect of mass hysteria, encouraged by a weak and evil governor. But the philosopher Emperor seems to have done nothing to protect the sufferers. Where he speaks in his personal memoirs of the Christians it is with a total lack of sympathy or insight that is quite shocking. They are brave, but their bravery is blind obstinacy, not worthy to be compared with the high courage of a Stoic sage. We see here that extreme, almost unconscious, pride, which I suggested in a past lecture to have been the besetting sin of the Stoic. There is a curious legend that during the Northern wars Marcus's army was relieved of drought by a sudden miraculous rain and that a storm following discomfited the enemy; this was the result of the prayers of a legion, Christian in composition, from Melitene—the ' thundering ' legion. Unfortunately the epithet *fulminata* is certainly of earlier date. The ' miracle ' however certainly took place; it is suggested by a scene on the column of Marcus, with Jupiter Pluvius shedding healing showers on the Romans, and by imperial coins, which preserve the pagan version of the event—that it was produced by an Egyptian magician, Arnuphis, the minister of Thoth, the Egyptian Mercury. Commodus, the degenerate son of Marcus, declined from old Roman discipline, lived like an Eastern sultan—and incidentally showed a keen interest in Eastern religions. Through his concubine, Marcia, a Christian, he learned to have kindlier feelings for the faith and relieved the sufferings of some exiles. It is only partially true that good Emperors do not persecute and bad Emperors do. Persecution sprang largely out of such worthy motives as the desire to protect the old Roman ways from dangerous innovations. Mercy to Christians might be only a sign of a weakness of character. Under Septimius Severus (A.D. 193-211) there was a new prohibition against becoming a Christian—aimed, that is to say, against the increase of the body. But the women of the house of Severus, Julia Domna, Julia Maesa and Julia Mammaea, of the royal priestly family of Emesa, had wide religious sympathies. Julia Mammaea, the mother of the gentle Severus Alexander (A.D. 222-235), actually met and conversed with the great Origen. Whether Severus Alexander himself really kept an image of Christ in his chapel, as the *Life* tells us, must be left doubtful; there is in it much romancing amid a little history. It is certain that a dynasty, deeply interested in Eastern religions, did not share the old Roman aversion to Christianity. The giant barbarian, Maximin the First, who succeeded Alexander (A.D. 235), loved the army and hated everyone else—the senate, the rich, the civilians generally. The Christians came under this inclusive hatred. Philip the Arabian (A.D. 244-249) was married to a Christian wife, Otacilia Severa, and was himself not unfriendly to the Church. Pagans complained of a lack of enthusiasm when he celebrated the thousandth year of Rome. He did not exploit it to the full for the honour of the old gods. Philip's successor, Decius, raised up against him by the armies of the Danube, claimed to be a second Trajan, destined to restore Roman *virtus* and crush the weak elements that threatened it. His reign was spent in desperate struggles against Kniva and his Goths, and he died a hero's death on the lost field of Abrittus (A.D. 251). But he found time before he died to set on foot the first general persecution of the Christians. He did not aim directly at them; all subjects of the Empire were required to present certificates to the effect that they were in the habit of sacrificing to the gods. A number of such certificates survive from Egypt. This was a net with meshes too fine to let Christians through. They must either suffer for their faith or sacrifice or, at least, produce a certificate to say that they had sacrificed. Very many of the weaker brethren lapsed. So much for the negative side of Decius's action. But what was he trying positively to effect? A restoration of vitality to the old paganism, the worship of the great gods of the State? The coins of Decius give a surprisingly definite answer to this question. They have less than the average reign to say of the State gods; but they *do* include a whole gallery of the *divi*, the Emperors consecrated for meritorious service and enshrined in the imperial heaven; the date of these coins is now certain. It was to this worship of the imperial gods that Decius wished to direct his subjects. It is the State that matters; the gods concern him as protectors of the imperial order. The persecution of Decius just lasted into the reign of Trebonianus Gallus his successor. It was revived with serious purpose by Valerian (A.D. 253-258-9). The blow was aimed this time at the heads of the churches, the bishops. But then came the incredible disaster—the capture of an Emperor by the Persian king (A.D. 258-259)—to the pagans an unintelligible misfortune for a noble man, to the Christians a manifest sign of divine judgement on the persecutor. How Gallienus, the son who survived Valerian, gave the Church peace for over a generation will concern us in our next lecture.

The period that we have been discussing has a certain unity. Throughout the whole of it the Empire is at war with the Church. At first it is a cold war, waged intermittently and without very purposeful direction. Towards the close the war becomes hot; it is directed from the centre and aims at the vital spots of the Church. The change from cold to hot will be better understood if we glance at the growth and development of the Church in the interval.

The Empire had begun by hardly seeing the Christians. Then for a long time it regarded them as something undesirable, a nuisance to be abated when it forced itself upon your notice, but not as a serious menace. The Church profited by this lack of resolute policy to grow in numbers and influence and to perfect its organization. For a long time still the Christians were to be no more than a vigorous minority. But the African barrister, Tertullian, can boast that there is no province, no class into which the Christians have not penetrated, that, if they withdrew, they would leave the Empire depopulated. The government of the Churches grew stronger than before; the bishop, the chief of the overseers, acquired his monarchical position. The Bishop of Rome came to enjoy a special prestige in his central seat; by the middle of the third century there was some question of making him the referee in matters of dispute. That is not to say that the evidence for a ' Pope ' in the early Church is clear enough to convince the unconverted. But, when temporal appeals went to Rome, it was natural enough to think of sending to Rome spiritual appeals too.

The Christian duty of brotherly love was taken seriously and carried over into practice. Christianity came to be a Friendly Society of extraordinary scope and power. Unobserved by the Roman government, much of Roman *gravitas* and *virtus* was built into the framework of the Church. The Church was, in fact, coming to be a state within the State. The Empire, slow to recognize what was happening, struck hard at last—but too late. But the charity of the Church was not more important than its discipline. A Christian lived in a community which set high standards before its members and expected them to live up to them. The test came in the persecutions of Decius and his successors. Very large numbers had lapsed—had sacrificed or secured certificates to say that they had. How was the Church to treat them, when the strain relaxed and they asked to be taken back? To readmit the lapsed too readily would have meant a fatal slackening of discipline; to close the door against the penitent would have cost the Church too much blood. A judicious blend of severity and mercy was achieved. Forgiveness, after repentance attested by heavy penance, was the rule. It is curious that the authorities, the bishops, usually stood out against too ready leniency, while the confessors, those who had suffered for their faith, were quick to excuse and intercede for the fallen. The blend of mercy and justice was triumphantly successful.

45

If Christianity, living in a world organized by Rome, learned to absorb much of Roman practical genius, so too, living in a world interpreted by Greek thought, it learned to find its right relation to Greek philosophy. In the second to third centuries Clement of Alexandria and the greater Origen found a new interpretation of the faith that might appeal to men who knew their Plato. Christianity ceased to be an intellectual freak. Having to live on in the world it began to draw to itself such already existing elements as it could assimilate. In its encounters with the thought of the age—with Greek philosophy and, beside it, Oriental speculations—the Church had to steer its way through passages sown with rocks. A crop of heresies, usually classed together as Gnostic, though very various in character, came up like mushrooms. They revealed esoteric interpretations of the faith, not known to the vulgar. They were distinguished by luxuriant fancy and often by overweening spiritual pride. Marcion, with his god of the Old Testament distinct from the God of the new, Valentinus with his strange, mystical fancies of the *pleroma* or *pleromata* of divine essences, may stand as representatives of the rest. St. Paul, by the way, uses the word, *pleroma,* ' the fulness of the Godhead '— with how much of the Gnostic meaning who can say? Through these perilous passages the Church safely made her way. She held fast to her core of sacred mystery, but rejected all these additions of the rioting intellect. It was in the struggle against these heresies that the Creed must slowly have advanced towards formulation. Schism, as distinct from heresy, was not so common. The one well-known example is that of the Montanists, which rose in Phrygia in the second half of the second century and for a long time had wide influence. The Montanists claimed to live still under the direct guidance of the Holy Spirit. They inclined to veneration of prophets and prophetesses, to extreme rigour of life and to some degree of disobedience to Church discipline. The great apologist, Tertullian, became a Montanist and his later writings are coloured by his choice.

The early Christian writings had been meant for the faithful. St. Paul wrote to instruct his Churches; the Gospels formulated for Christians the kind of teaching that had formed the basis of instruction for catechumens. The Gospel of Luke and the Acts perhaps show some interest in possible readers from outside. In this second period Christianity addresses itself to the world in which it lives. A series of Apologists, Aristides, Justin Martyr and the rest, write defences of the faith, clearing it of false charges and explaining what its real bents and aims are. These Apologies may actually be addressed to reigning Emperors. Trajan and Hadrian had mitigated the severity of the law by leniency in its application and it might be hoped that a better knowledge of Christianity would lead to a more real toleration. Whether the Emperors addressed paid any attention to these appeals cannot be known; no fruit appears in action. One simple and delightful explanation of Christianity for the general public, it seems, has come down to us in the *Octavius* of Minucius Felix. There were not wanting answers from the pagan side. One, Celsus, known to us fairly fully from Origen's confutation of his arguments, pointed out what seemed to him to be the fatal weaknesses of Christianity: but he recognized some strength and goodness in it, for he earnestly appealed to Christians not to withdraw their services from a hardly pressed Empire that needed them.

With Tertullian, the able, bitter, eloquent African barrister, we meet a new note, a note of anger and defiance. The Christians are now too many and too influential to be despised and trodden down. Their doctrine and practice are too pure for unscrupulous attack. What sort of criminals are those who are to be suppressed mercilessly, if found, but are not to be sought out? The fact is, the Christians are made the universal scapegoats, whenever anything goes wrong. And so attention is diverted from the real causes of miseries—which, if understood, might be cured. Mobs are in their nature stupid and irresponsible; but it is a disgrace for a government to leave the decision of important matters to their base instincts and the caprice of evil or spineless governors. Tertullian is too bitter to convert enemies, but his case against the Empire is really unanswerable and was in the end admitted by the Empire itself. It condemned the impossible middle way. It first tried, with Decius, Valerian and Diocletian, the war to the knife. It then admitted, with Constantine the Great, that, if the Church could not be extirpated, it must be taken into partnership with the Empire.

Christianity was lodged in the Empire as a foreign body, making some attempts to accommodate itself to its environment, but too sure of itself to make all the adaptation unless the Empire were willing to come some of the way to meet it. What were the main points of conflict?

The first, of course, was the religious. Worshipping One God the Christians made void the many gods of the pagans. This led on naturally to the belief that those gods were angry at neglect and showed their wrath by strange and awful visitations. The realization that such visitations were not limited to Christian times and places must slowly have exposed the falsity of this argument. The Christians could not well retaliate; for their God of Love must not be vindictive. Yet we shall find some Christians gloating over the horrible end of Galerius. An event like the captivity of Valerian must have made a deep impression on many pagans, without any need for Christians to rub it in.

Next to the religious difficulty came the social and moral. The Christian questioned much that seemed acceptable to the average pagan. It was not only over grave moral issues that the trouble came. Such a simple matter as the wearing of a wreath at a banquet might be too much for the conscience of some. The refusal of Christians to participate in the brutality of gladiatorial shows or in the immorality of the theatre was morally unquestionable; but it gave deep offence. The public baths—not baths only, but social clubs as well—were suspect to the Christians, because they often encouraged lax morals. From this aspect of the baths comes that association of holiness with unwashenness in so much early Christian thought.

A very serious objection urged by thoughtful pagans against the Church was that, by overvaluing virginity, it lowered the status of marriage and tended to reduce the birth-rate. We should like to know if the birth-rate among Christians was actually lower than that among pagans. In the first age, when the Second Coming of Christ was urgently expected, marriage might appear a very temporary affair. But things were changed when the millennial hope was transferred to a distant future and, for as long ahead as you could see, the Roman Empire was the home for Christians on earth. Even if fewer children were born to Christian parents—and that is not by any means certain—the deficiency would probably be made up by the refusal of Christians to expose children as unwanted. Normally all children born would be reared.

Christianity was a religion of peace, with the peace of God in its heart. The Empire too rested on the Augustan peace—and so far the two might seem to agree. But the peace of the Empire was an armed peace; order must be maintained at home; the frontiers must be defended against the barbarians. The Christian might be expected to be reluctant to join the army, and, if the Christians continually grew in numbers, this reluctance might be serious for the Empire. It is hard to judge where the truth lies. Undoubtedly, the early Church, as a persecuted minority, was more ' pacifist ' than a Church incorporated in a State can ever be. Many Christians would hold that there were better things for them to do than to serve in the army. But Christian soldiers there certainly were—even if the Christian soldiers of the hymn wage only spiritual warfare. There was never any question of declaring the profession of arms closed to a Christian. As a matter of fact, in all the older and more settled provinces there was a growing reluctance among all classes to volunteer for military service; the burden of imperial defence was shifted largely on to barbarian shoulders, and this led in the end to the barbarization of the Roman army. The Christians, then, were made to bear the sole blame for a process by no means limited to them.

The struggle between Church and Empire reached its climax in Confession and Martyrdom, when the Christian, face to face with authority, confessed his faith by suffering or sealed it by his blood. It was only right and natural that the Christians should honour their heroes and heroines; and, as the rage of the adversary often extended to the bodies of the dead, so the Church extended its honour to the sacred remains. Such was the decent and reasonable origin of that veneration of relics which reached such grisly developments in later history. The vast literature of the *Acta Martyrum,* still being edited by the Bollandists, contains material of very various value—stories of heroic endurance, horrific pictures of tortures and miracles galore. It is not difficult as a rule to separate the wheat from the chaff. Shorthand records of trials were, we know, taken down; and our accounts often follow a clear-cut form, which we have every reason to accept as the normal one. The governor, interrogating the prisoner, is concerned first to get his full confession; secondly, equally concerned to persuade him, if necessary by torture, to recant and accept pardon. The Christian who endures to the end begrudges his interrogator this coveted triumph. The beauty of the noblest stories of martyrdom speaks for itself. We think of Bishop Polycarp refusing to curse the Christ who has been his friend for eighty-six years; of St. Perpetua and St. Felicitas, matron and slave-girl, exchanging the last kiss of peace in the arena; of the great-souled Blandina, the slave who tired out her torturers at Lugdunum; of Bishop Cyprian, receiving the death sentence with his *Deo gratias*—thanks to God, as ever, so now for this His final dispensation. The horrors of torture were not imaginary; paganism was very harsh and merciless against offenders against its codes. *Christiani ad leones, Christianae ad lenones*—the terrible cry was heard again and again. Honour as well as life was ruthlessly sacrificed. But morbid interest in horrors tends to lower the real glory of the martyrs. Of miracles it is hard to judge. Natural events might be so ordered that escape came from the seemingly impossible position. Miracles of courageous endurance, inspired by grace, there certainly were. Miracles in the sense of suspension of the ordinary laws of nature—many find these very hard to credit; and yet, I think, we are not so assured in our incredulity as we were.

Not all the martyrs were of the genuine, the noble type. There were excitable, ill-balanced persons, who rushed rashly into peril—only to be sorry when it was too late. There were men of blind, stupid courage—the sort of courage which Marcus Aurelius thought to be characteristic of the Christians—who were driven by a passion for exhibitionism—for showing off, to use a simpler phrase—to challenge authority. The great wit, Lucian, gives a portrait of a man of this type, Peregrinus. But the true martyr did not run on death. He tried to live his life in peace; if danger threatened, he might withdraw for the time before it; but, finally, if the test came, he would not renounce his Master, but would trust the final issue to Him.

In the period which we have been considering, the fight between Church and Empire may already have been decided. The critical moment may have passed, the moment when the Church could conceivably have been crushed. The only policy remaining for the Empire may have been acceptance. The third race—third after the pagans and the Jews—may have taken root too deep to be removed. If that was so, it was not realized yet on the side of the Empire, perhaps not on that of the Church even. The next period, c. A.D. 258 to 312, was to make clear the victory of the Church, its nature and its extent.

CHAPTER 5

THE CHURCH AND THE EMPIRE:
GALLIENUS TO CONSTANTINE
THE GREAT

We have already seen how the Roman government early adopted a hostile attitude towards the Christians; how, without real toleration, some respite was given by Emperors who discouraged persecution; how the Church, taking advantage of the intermittency of the attacks, grew in numbers and in strength of organization. For a long time the government seems to have no serious reason for persecution; the mob may hate the Christians for their peculiarities, their refusal to share in many of the amenities of life, a governor may here and there throw a few Christians to the mob. But what serious danger lies in them? By the time that we have now reached, that is all changed. The Christians are now a real menace; the Church, if not broken, seems like to overcome the Empire. Decius struck hard—but without final success; Valerian soon renewed his attack, with more finesse, aiming at the heads of the Church. The Empire was falling on evil days; the great crisis was upon it—barbarian invasions, rebellions in the provinces, collapse of the currency. Imperial propaganda might still speak of an age of gold; for many, for the Christians in particular, it was an age of iron. For all the misfortunes of the Empire were laid to their account.

The capture of Valerian by the Persians must have come as a terrible shock to Rome. His son, his colleague, who survived him—Gallienus—reversed his father's policy and allowed what amounted to toleration. Gallienus was not the weakling that he appears in some histories. He never despaired—not when the West seceded under its own Gallic Emperors, not when the East set up its rival Emperors, not when the Palmyrenes, having helped Rome to drive back the Persian, Sapor, began to claim something like independence for themselves, not when the Goths, descending from the Black Sea, carried havoc far and wide. It is quite possible that by the time of Gallienus's death, A.D. 268, the worst was over, that his officers who murdered him were really wasting a crime.

In such parts of the Empire as still acknowledged his rule Gallienus seems to have presented himself as a prince of peace. The toleration granted to the Christians would fit in well with this general policy. Strength was to be found in concord at home, until the Fortune of Rome had had time to repair the losses abroad. Gallienus was certainly no Christian himself; his serious interest was in philosophy; he was a patron of the great Plotinus. But the Empress, Salonina, was a Christian. Coins of hers from the mint of Milan show a female figure, bearing the branch of peace, with the legend, AVGVSTA IN PACE—far too Christian in tone to be possible, unless the Empress herself approved.

After the death of Gallienus, the crisis of the Empire soon passed. Claudius Gothicus broke the Goths; his successor, Aurelian, restored the unity of the Empire and set the currency again on a firm base. Another great Emperor, Probus (A.D. 276-282), confirmed and strengthened the new won peace. When at last in A.D. 283 the Empire found in Diocletian a head that could plan as well as a hand that could strike, the hour was ripe for reform or restoration everywhere. Under new forms the Empire was to enter on a new lease of life Meanwhile the peace of the Church continued. Aurelian is credited in his last years with the intention of renewing the persecution; the intention, if it existed, was frustrated by the officers who conspired to murder him. On one occasion he was called in to arbitrate in Church affairs. The able, but irregular, Paul of Samosata was contesting with a rival the bishopric of Antioch. Appeal was made to Aurelian, who was in the East fighting Palmyra, and he gave the decision in favour of Paul's rival, because he had the support of Rome. Aurelian here appears rather as a forerunner of Constantine than of Diocletian.

The reforms of Diocletian extended to all departments of life. To us they appear more drastic than they really were, for, in many cases, they only recognized changes which were already near completion. But, even so, they were drastic enough. Diocletian made an end of the *princeps* and replaced him by a *dominus et deus,* a semi-divine king like the Persian. With himself he associated a comrade in arms, Maximian, as joint Emperor; in A.D. 293 he gave himself and his colleague a junior assistant each, a Cæsar, and so created his famous Tetrarchy, a team of four governing the Empire in four great sections. Diocletian reduced the size and increased the number of the provinces; he likewise reduced the size and increased the number of the legions. He may have begun to create a field army beside the frontier ones. He made permanent that division between civil and military career, which had long been growing and had reached something of a climax under Gallienus. He reorganized the system of taxation and reformed the coinage. Rome lost her old supremacy and became just one of a number of imperial capitals. In this new form the Empire might prolong its days; but much of the old Roman ideal was lost for ever; the word 'liberty' had little meaning left. The burden of the army and civil service, heavy even in time of peace, became unendurable in war; the taxes could only be collected by brutal oppression. Society was frozen in a system of castes; while slavery diminished, serfdom increased. The local senators, bowed down under the load of collecting the taxes, tried at all costs to escape from their honorary bondage. This flight from the senates, the *curiae,* was just one example of the attempt to escape from a frame of life more and more predestined by the State. This age of extreme regimentation was assuredly no easy one to live in.

The age was one of faith; men at large believed in divine powers who manifested themselves in human affairs. The only question was, who those powers were. We shall be completely wrong if we imagine that even the most seasoned politicians of the time were religiously indifferent. The

Christian Church, having mastered the Gnostics, was beginning to define its Creed. The pagans may have been advancing to new interpretations, to new forms of belief; but so far from being dead, paganism was receiving reinforcement from the successors of Plotinus, the Neo-Pythagoreans, who supplied mystical explanations of popular religion. In the East the dualism of Mani was thriving mightily. Diocletian could not be indifferent to the religious problem. Gallienus had found a formula for the moment, not a final settlement. What was to be the religion of the reformed Empire?

Early in his reign Diocletian produced a new version of pagan belief. He put himself under the special protection of Jupiter, while Maximian similarly claimed Hercules as his protector. Diocletian *(Iovius)* was not Jupiter, Maximian *(Herculius)* was not Hercules; but each stood very near his god; perhaps, the correct Roman expression would be that Jupiter was the spirit, the *genius,* of the senior Emperor, Hercules of the junior. Outwardly the peace of Gallienus continued. But about A.D. 296 a purge of Christians from army and Civil Service began—an ominous sign for the future; in 303 the Great Persecution broke out.

How is this development to be interpreted? Can we be wrong in thinking that the new system of Diocletian, Jupiter, god the father, Hercules, god the son, was intended to resolve the current disharmonies? If we turn to Arnobius, the apologist of the age of the persecution, we find the stress falling all on the Father and the Son; of God the Holy Spirit there is no clear teaching. On several occasions Arnobius, in defending the Christian belief in Christ, uses the analogy of pagan gods, and in particular of Hercules. Diocletian had Christians among his personal servants; his wife and daughter were both Christians. He may have known just sufficient of the Faith to imagine that his system of Father and Son might be near enough to these troublesome people to win at least their tacit acceptance. Had all pagans been as politic as Diocletian, we can imagine that an advance might have been made along his lines—though no faithful Christian, however moderate, would have finally acquiesced in the substitution for Christianity of a slightly modified form of paganism. This question never arose. The pagan side had its zealots, men who believed passionately in the old order and who laid on the Church the blame for all Rome's sufferings. Chief among these was Galerius, Cæsar of Diocletian in the East, an able general, growing every year in power. We seem to see his hand in the purge of an army and civil service. The Great Persecution of A.D. 303 was probably entirely his work—the bloody persecution without any doubt so.

The attack was launched with considerable skill. First came the impugning of the loyalty of Christians in the imperial services. Then the oracles were consulted and gave the expected answers, very damaging to the 'impious'. The soothsayers complained to Diocletian that the answers of the gods in the entrails of beasts could no longer be read correctly, because of the presence of 'righteous' persons— that is to say, of Christians who protected themselves from contamination by making the saving sign of the Holy Cross.

In A.D. 303 Diocletian gave in; we imagine him struggling for a time to maintain his first policy of conciliation. War was declared on the Church. The attack was conducted on the lines laid down by Decius and Valerian, but it was now more violent and more general. Churches were to be destroyed, the sacred Scriptures burnt, the persons of the bishops secured. It was at Nicomedia that the persecution was first announced. At this precise moment the imperial palace there was burned down. It may have been accident, but the blame was laid on the Christians, and the persecution moved forward with a rush. Perhaps Galerius and his friends engineered an accident, which suited their plans, much as the burning of the Reichstag suited Hitler's Nazis. Diocletian himself intended to stop short of bloodshed; but he was incapacitated for months by a severe nervous breakdown, no doubt brought on by the strain of action that struck so many near to him, and, by the time that he recovered, the mischief was done. The bloody persecution was in full course. In A.D. 305, Diocletian, and with him, Maximian, abdicated. Nominally it was an act of supreme wisdom and self-abnegation on the part of two Elder States-men; in fact, Galerius left him no choice. The new Tetrarchy was Galerius's: true, Constantius, Augustus of the West, was senior Emperor and could not be got rid of; but the two new Cæsars, Severus and Maximin Daza, were both Galerius's men—and not much else; Constantine, son of Constantius, and Maxentius, son of Maximian, were both passed over. It is impossible here to recount in full the complicated history of the years A.D. 305 to 311, impossible too not to give some short account of them. Constantius died in 306; Constantine, who had escaped from the court of Galerius a few months earlier, was acclaimed Augustus by his troops. Galerius, most unwillingly, conceded to him the second rank of Cæsar, which Constantine wisely accepted. In 306 Maxentius was made Emperor by the praetorian guard in Rome; his father, Maximian, came back from abdication to assist him. First, Severus, Augustus of the West after Constantius, then Galerius himself failed to put down the pretender. A tricky game of power politics followed—with as many as six Augusti at one time claiming to hold power simultaneously. The Tetrarchy of Diocletian had disappeared, and that firm basis from which the persecution had been launched was there no more. When Galerius, in his desperate illness, at last granted toleration, he will have been moved by the uncertainties of the political situation as well as by the failure of his religious policy on its own ground.

The last great battle of the Church with the Empire has been described for us with intense power by Lactantius, later to be tutor of Constantine's eldest son. He relates with effect, and some glee, the awful ends of the persecutors. The persecution raged over most of the Empire, most furiously in the East. In the West Constantius kept it within limits. For the moment the Church was defeated, its organization shattered, its leaders dispersed. Many of its best were martyred, only too many fell away. But the hope and faith of the Church lived on underground and many pagans sickened of the bloodshed; they often tried to save martyrs even against their will. Galerius on his death-bed, ' eaten by worms ', according to the ancient diagnosis, revoked his own decrees. He granted liberty of worship to the Christians—albeit with no change of heart and with angry reluctance—and bade them pray for his recovery. Soon afterwards he died.

The persecution, then, was at an end, abandoned by the prime mover, and him now dead. The future depended mainly on the personality of Constantine, the son of Constantius. His father had been known as a ruler of wise and gentle character, moderate in religion and, though not a Christian, a monotheist. Constantine was a man of vast mental and physical energy, a fine general, an able diplomatist, intensely ambitious. He was a man of faith and something of a visionary. In his pagan days his chief reverence was for Apollo, or the Sun-god, if you chose to emphasize that side of his activities.

Constantine had been deeply impressed by the courage of the Christians and came under the influence of a remarkable personality, Bishop Hosius of Corduba. He gradually arrived at the conviction that it was in the Christian God and his Christ that the *virtus,* the power which he had been wont to ascribe to Apollo and the other pagan gods, really resided.

With Galerius dead, there remained four Augusti— Constantine in the West, Licinius in the Balkans, now leaning to alliance with Constantine; Maxentius in Rome and Maximin Daza in the East, the last two drawing together against the other two. Constantine resolved to win back Rome and Italy from Maxentius. Maxentius was not notorious as a persecutor, but Constantine made his campaign a test of the help of the Christian God. As he told Eusebius he had seen a vision in the night sky—a cross of light and round it the words, ' in this sign you shall conquer ', τούτῳ νίκα, *hoc signo victor eris.* He marked the sign of the cross on the shields of his men—we can only guess what they made of it—attacked Rome and conquered. Soon after this victory, the battle of the Mulvian Bridge, Maximin attacked Licinius, was defeated and died a little later. Maximin had continued the persecution in the East with some

59

adroitness, trying to disparage the Christian cause by propaganda and to rouse paganism to some emulation of the strong points of the Church. With his death all was over. Constantine and Licinius reaffirmed in the Edict of Milan the toleration conceded by Galerius. For a time Constantine and Licinius ruled together, in West and East respectively. But causes of dispute arose and finally in A.D. 324 Licinius was defeated and, after a short reprieve, put to death. In his last fight with Constantine he reverted to paganism and tried to rally the pagans of the East in his cause. The Empire was once more united under one head, and that head was Constantine.

The triumph of Christianity did not depend only on the personality of Constantine. The Church could not be ignored; if it could not be broken, it must be given its place in the Empire. Even Galerius had been brought to admit this. But the precise way in which the great change was made *did* depend on Constantine. Adroit and unscrupulous as he could be in his statesmanship, he was sincerely convinced, genuinely converted; he did not become a Christian for policy. No doubt, his apprehension of Christian philosophy was feeble, his loyalty to its morality not always enlightened; but, in that, he was only representative of the masses who joined the Church, now that it was an object of imperial favour; they would carry over with them as much of their paganism as they could. The letters of Constantine, certainly genuine, as is now generally allowed, convey an unmistakeable impression of a powerful personality, labouring under the stress of new experiences and emotions. Later pagans asserted that Constantine only became a Christian after the terrible domestic tragedy, in which first his son Crispus, then his wife, Fausta, perished (A.D. 326); only the Christian God, they said, offered pardon for crimes like that. This was a silly lie. The critical change in Constantine took place many years before that. If he deferred baptism to his death-bed he was only taking a reasonable precaution, taken by many; for sins after baptism were judged to be too heinous to be washed out by anything but the blood of martyrdom.

The Church, till now an object of fear and hatred, becomes an object of imperial protection and favour. It receives back its confiscated property, swelled by munificent gifts from the Emperor. Bishops are held in the highest honour and travel at the public expense. Confessors receive the Emperor's kiss—no mere mark of sentiment, but a sign of admission to the inner ring of imperial favour. Constantine, we know, did not make over to the Church the heritage of the Roman Empire in the West. But he *did* take those first steps towards building up its prestige to the point from which, when the Western Emperor was gone, the Bishop of Rome stepped almost automatically into his place.

Constantine was undoubtedly inspired by the hope that the united Church would make an admirable partner for his united Empire. He soon found to his dismay that the Church was not so united after all. He felt also that he had a special responsibility laid on him. The Bishops were the natural leaders of the Church within; as such he paid them the highest honours. But a function remained for him himself; he was the Bishop of those who were without— of subjects not yet in the fold. His first trouble was with the Donatists in Africa, wild enthusiasts who took a most unfavourable view of any who had lapsed under persecution. Constantine set himself, without any lasting success, to bring these troublesome people back into submission to Church discipline. Even more serious was the second enemy that confronted him—heresy in the form of Arianism, a denial of the full divinity of the Son of God. At the Council of Nicaea Constantine was finally presented with a complete affirmation of the Athanasian Creed of God in Three Persons—the Son of the same substance, not of like substance, with the Father (ὁμοούσιος not ὁμοιούσιος) Constantine certainly desired Church unity above all. For the philosophy of the dispute he had little understanding and allowed modifications of the formulary to be suggested, which made it easier for the moment for some waverers to conform, but embittered the conflict for the next generation.

The victory over the persecution had been attested by the concession of toleration in religious matters. Toleration, thus won for the Christian, could not be at once denied to the pagan. Constantine made no secret of his own conviction that the truth was in Christianity, of his own deep wish that all men should come to acknowledge it. But meanwhile men, sunk so deep in ignorance and blindness, must be treated gently, till they awake from their errors. Scholars differ in their estimate of the extent to which Constantine himself damaged paganism. Some acts of repression there certainly were, directed against pagan seats of worship, notorious for their immorality, or against such evil practices as magic. But whether Constantine intended to proceed to a direct assault on the old religion is matter of dispute.

The coins throw interesting light on the way in which the new age revealed its changed character. The pagan deities ceased to appear on the coins of Constantine after 312. All except the Sun-god, *Sol invictus comes;* he lasts on for some five years or more, and has occasionally a Christian symbol, cross or monogram of Christ, at his side. Constantine had, as we have seen, adored the pagan Apollo, or Sol, in his early days. He seems for a time to have associated his old faith with his new—as if Apollo could suggest Christ, ' the Son of Righteousness '. Or was he consciously aiming at a neutrality in religion? The withdrawal of the Sol types, soon after 317, seems to prove that this attempt at harmony of old and new was unsuccessful. For the future the gods never revisit the coins. The themes are now the exploits of the Emperor and his sons, their victories, their vows—not unconnected in many cases with the old paganism, but not offensively ostentatious of it. The only Christian type is the exceptional *labarum* (imperial standard with the monogram of Christ) set on the ancient serpent—*Spes Publica,* ' the hope of the State '. There are no types of Jesus Christ or of the Virgin Mary or of any Saint. Even the cross and the monogram of Christ only appear occasionally and as minor adjuncts of the type, symbols as we call them. Even these symbols were not placed there without authority; they could not have been tolerated, unless the Emperor himself had favoured Christianity. But the small place that they take up witnesses in this special case to that toleration which Constantine had accepted for the pagans too. The coins, like the literature of the age, use by preference formulae of a general character which could be interpreted at will in a Christian or in a pagan sense. For a season there was an armistice after battle.

Constantinople, the new Byzantium, also called the new Rome, built between A.D. 326 and 330 in its unrivalled position at the mouth of the Black Sea, was from the first planned as a Christian city. Old Rome remained stubbornly, if not defiantly, pagan. Yet even here there were ambiguous signs. Constantine consulted pagan magicians as to the auspicious hour for dedication. The Genius, Tyche, of the new city, Ἀνθοῦσα, was represented in the characteristic garb of a city Fortune. A colossal statue of Constantine himself, wearing the rays of the Sun-god, bore the inscription Κωνσταντίνου λάμποντος Ἡλίου δίκην.

Christianity had long been in conflict with the world on matters of individual conduct and belief. The struggle did not stop because it was now to be fought out inside, not outside, the Church. The *interpretatio Romana* had already been applied to many religions not Roman; it would now be applied, if might be, to Christianity. On the moral side, too, Christian ethic would be open to attack, not by avowed enemies, but by converts who continued to live by their old standards.

And there was one point more. Christianity had so far known the State as a persecutor, or, at least, a disinterested protector of it as a part of Society. It was now brought into an intimate alliance. Christians were now being appointed to important posts of confidence. The arbitration of Bishops was recognized as legal, when sought by both parties in a dispute. With Constantine favouring the Church to the extent that he did, no clear dividing line could be drawn between Church and public affairs. Under these circumstances Christianity must both influence, and undergo influence itself. In legislation traces of Christian temper are occasionally to be seen. For the most part, the terrible, often stupid, harshness of the criminal law persists. The worst abuses—the corruption and venality in the close entourage of the Emperor, the merciless grinding of the tax machine—continued with little sign of improvement. After all, the State had its long development behind it; with all its grave faults it had its virtues too; it had acquired a sense of the possible—not of the best that might be done, but of the little that might at least be realized. It was inevitable that in the new partnership the Church received as well as gave.

The reign of Constantine has brought us to the great divide—the crossing from paganism to Christianity. Our last lecture will follow the history of Church and Empire, in the generations following. We shall see what the fruits of victory were.

CHAPTER 6

THE CHRISTIAN EMPIRE

As long as Constantine lived his personality was the determining factor in the course taken by events. After he had died in the spotless white robe of the Christian novice and been buried in his own city beside the tombs of the twelve Apostles, as the thirteenth of their number, himself ἰσαπόστολος, the world was left to face the problems created by his decisive actions. There were three sons of Constantine surviving—Constantine II, perhaps the issue of a morganatic union with a lady of Arles, Constantius II and Constans, sons of the unhappy Fausta. Constantine II had received a training in war and statecraft such as had not fallen to his two younger brothers and it seems certain that the father must have intended him to hold a sort of Presidency in the imperial college, the more so as, beside his sons, he appointed two cousins, Delmatius and Hannibalianus, to command on the Danube and in Armenia respectively. But within a few months of the death of Constantine the troops in Constantinople rose and massacred these two princes together with most members of the side branch of the house, deriving from the half-brothers and sisters of the old Emperor. Only sons of the Great were to succeed him. Constantius II was guilty at least of condoning the horrible act. Julian the Apostate, a baby at the time, was one of the few to be spared; he never forgot or forgave the ruin of his family.

The sons of Constantine met and made a new division of the Empire. But the seeds of discord had been sown. Constantine II tried to assert a suzerainty over Constans and was killed in the attempt. Constantius was left to rule in the East, Constans in the West. Both of course were Christians, but, while Constantius favoured the Arians,

Constans had given refuge to the exiled patriarch, Athanasius, and supported his cause. Constans for a time enjoyed more freedom of movement than Constantius, who was hampered by a dragging war with Persia, and gained successes against barbarian enemies. But in A.D. 350 he was murdered by a rival, Magnentius, to whom the West soon fell away. With great difficulty Constantius mastered this formidable foe and reigned over an Empire, again united. But he needed assistants in his task and was forced to look for them among the few survivors from the blood bath of 337—first, Constantius Gallus III, A.D. 351-354, then Julian, A.D. 355 to 360. But the blood fury of the house was not yet at rest. Gallus fell victim to suspicions of disloyalty and was executed. Julian, in his turn, pressed to assume the title of Augustus by his troops, was forced into rebellion; the civil war was only terminated by the death of Constantius from natural causes in 361.

This period, 337 to 360, was marked—or shall we say disgraced?—by a series of great Church Councils, concerned mainly with the interminable dispute about the Person of Christ. The conflict went in favour of the Athanasians, while Constans lived; after his death it turned decidedly against them. We should be most unjust to the Fathers of this generation if we treated the whole discussion as a mere splitting of hairs—if we missed its real importance—was the Christian faith to retain its own sacred mysteries or was it to become a special form of revised paganism? The barbarian peoples, notably the Goths, accepted Christianity by preference in its Arian form; this in itself suggests strongly that Arianism was near to pagan ways of thought. We saw in the last lecture how Diocletian had already offered the scheme of the divine father, Jupiter, and his heroic son, Hercules, as a new appeal to dissentients. But there is something terrifying in the heat of the *odium theologicum* that was engendered. Even the great Athanasius himself, whose solitary stand more than once against the world must excite admiration, was the bitterest and most uncompromising of antagonists.

So deeply absorbed in doctrinal strife, the Church did less than she perhaps might have done to reform the State. The same bitter complaints could still be directed against the intriguing eunuchs round the Emperor's person, the ubiquitous secret agents, the merciless tax-collectors. Nor was the fight against paganism pressed home; the armistice continued. The imperial coinage is not markedly Christian in tone. The pagan gods no longer appear, but many concepts of paganism, especially the minor deities, the 'Virtues', still hold their place—*Victoria, Virtus, Pax, Securitas, Spes.* Two definitely Christian types came out of the great civil war of 350-353. Vetranio, a general of Constantius, who for a short time assumed Empire in Illyricum and then laid it down at the feet of Constantius, struck a bronze coin, with the figure of the Emperor holding the *labarum* and legend, HOC SIGNO VICTOR ERIS—a new representation of the vision of Constantine the Great. Magnentius, the Western rebel, is recorded in history as a pagan; but his coins tell another story. He placed on a bronze coin the monogram of Christ with Alpha and Omega to left and right of it and the legend, SALVS DD NN AVG ET CAES, —a Christian coin and Christian in the Athanasian form. Magnentius probably turned that way in his last extremity and tried to enlist support against the Arian Constantius. Any reluctance of Christians to serve in the army was disappearing now that the Empire for which arms were born was itself Christian. The battle of Mursa, in which Constantius triumphed over Magnentius, was one of the bloodiest in Roman history; the followers of Magnentius, outnumbered and in the end outgeneralled, persisted for half a day in demonstrating a hopeless valour and selling their lives dear.

Julian II, known in history as the 'Apostate', was one of the most remarkable figures of his age. He was imbued with great traditions of the past, Roman *virtus* and *gravitas,* Greek humanism and philosophy. As a general he rendered gallant service against the German invaders of Gaul; he lost his life in an attempt to wrest the initiative from the Persians in the East. He strove hard and with some success to purify the administration. He had been brought up a Christian and knew Christianity from the inside; but his soul had been revolted by the massacre of 337. He saw in the new faith a wanton departure from tried norms of living. What was good in it belonged essentially to humanism and could be grafted on to a reformed paganism. Julian himself boasted of being a Greek philosopher, but his philosophy was shot through with religious mysticism, centred round the worship of the Sun-god. In his attacks on the Christian faith he deals some shrewd blows; but it is not unfair to say that, when he expounds his own mysticism, he is no less exposed to rationalistic attack. In the personality of Julian is contained the secret of his failure. Noble, individual, a trifle unbalanced, a trifle absurd, he was outside the main currents in which affection for the old paganism still ran strong—in Rome for example, still devoted to its past, its religion included. He found time in his short reign to prove his own enthusiasm for paganism, to show marked disfavour for Christians and to attempt to deny them a share in higher education—a silly piece of petulance, denounced even by pagans of the time. When he died things went back without a struggle to where they had been before him. His dying words, *Vicisti Galilaee,* whether or not spoken, tell the truth; he had pitted his own personality against the Saviour, and he had lost. He was too conscious of his own exceptional destiny and powers; he lacked appeal to the ordinary man. But his courage and moral worth impress us still; even a Christian poet, Prudentius, will not deny him his mead of praise;

perfidus ille Deo, sed non et perfidus orbi.

The coins of Julian show small sign of his reaction. They continue to use the neutral language about victories and vows, peace and hope. The one extraordinary type is that of the bull, Apis, with legend SECVRITAS REIPVBLICAE: a new appearance of the sacred animal was taken as a happy augury. The strange *Augustan History,* which is familiar enough with Christianity, but speaks of it without enthusiasm or with thinly veiled sarcasm, is probably of the age of Julian.

The successor chosen by the army to lead it back from Persia in 363 was Jovian, a Christian certainly, but no zealot, known for his affable manners. His successor after his short reign was Valentinian, a man of the same stamp, but of far more force. His main concern was the defence of the Empire against her barbarian invaders; at home he had the will, but not the power, to reform the worst abuses. In religion he maintained a toleration which appears to most modern judges as truly noble. Only at one point did he clash with paganism and its chief representatives, the aristocracy of Rome—in the trials for magic practices; these trials were directed against immoral or disloyal aims, but touched paganism, in so far as magic rites were a part of it.

Valentinian died in A.D. 375 and his sons, Gratian and Valentinian II, came in to rule beside Valens, brother of the elder Valentinian. In A.D. 378 the barbarian troubles culminated in the disaster of Adrianople. The Goths, pressed by the Huns, sought admission to the Empire as federate allies. Valens allowed them to cross the Danube, but they were swindled of money and supplies by the imperial officers and rose in revolt. Valens, with the flower of the army of the East, was ridden down by the Gothic cavalry. The Spaniard, Theodosius, called in by Gratian to repair the disaster, could only enlist Goths in mass in the imperial service; for a generation the army of the East was more Gothic than Roman.

Theodosius had been made Emperor by Gratian. When Gratian was killed in 383 by a British pretender, Magnus Maximus, Theodosius accepted the new colleague for a time. But when Maximus invaded Italy and drove out the younger Valentinian, Theodosius took up arms and destroyed the rebel. Valentinian, now really a ward of Theodosius, was put aside in 392 by the barbarian general, Arbogastes, who, however, instead of becoming Emperor himself, set up a Greek philosopher, Eugenius. Eugenius attempted to rally the forces of paganism and his struggle with Theodosius was generally accepted as a trial of strength between the old religion and the new. The victory of Theodosius at the river Frigidus, decided by a fierce wind which blew in the faces of the pagans, was judged to have settled the issue.

Under Theodosius Christianity in its most uncompromising form, the Athanasian, triumphed. The principle of toleration was abandoned. What was left of paganism was to be rooted out piece by piece. The influence on Theodosius of Ambrose, the great bishop of Milan, was decisive. After the terrible massacre which the Emperor in a fit of blind passion ordered at Thessalonica he was excluded by Ambrose from communion until he did penance for his sin. At this point our present inquiry stops. With the death of Theodosius and the accession of his sons, Arcadius in the East and Honorius in the West, the division of the Empire becomes permanent. The East survives its imminent dangers from Goths and Huns and goes forward to its long destiny as the Byzantine Empire. More and more it becomes a Christian State and Christian types take up the larger part of its coinage. The Western Empire lives on precariously for a few generations more, not decisively shattered by any one enemy, but slowly sapped by barbarian invasion, internal discord and the despair of subjects, ground between the upper and nether mill-stones—the rough and grasping invader and the heartless tax-collector.

The Church, as we have said, had now to face collective problems, not merely those of individual conduct. Influencing the State, it was itself seriously influenced by it. Many have queried with Dante, whether Constantine did not do more harm than good when he 'established' the Church. Money poured in, largely from the gifts of ladies of rank who left to the Church the wealth that was supposed to be reserved for their families. The splendour of the Pope, the Bishop of Rome, became so great that a pagan of high position could observe that he himself would not mind being Bishop at the price. The Church had from of old known three enemies, the world, the flesh and the devil. *Now* the first of these appeared more often as a friend—the more dangerous as such. Literature and art, always a little distrusted, are now drawn into the Christian current.

St. Jerome, conscience-stricken, laments that he is perhaps more a disciple of Cicero than of Christ.

Christianity from her early days had inherited the old treasures of Israel. She was now asked to assimilate the wealth of the cultures of Greece and Rome—of philosophy, statecraft, law. And a social change that had long been coming now reached completion—the religion of the poor and dispossessed became the religion of the rich and respectable. We probably underestimate the scope of the change here.

The struggle within the Church to establish and define her Creed went on for centuries. The general verdict today will be that it used up a vast amount of time and engendered a vast amount of bitterness. We will not call it desirable, are reluctant to admit it as necessary. It is easiest understood as one of the consequences of Establishment. An official Church finds it more important than before to define its position, and the prizes for the successful are correspondingly greater.

The change of attitude towards the pagans, the shift from toleration to proscription, may be accepted as inevitable. The balance once shifted must swing more and more to the stronger side. But opposition lingered on in some quarters. The city of Rome clung to its old traditions. The Roman nobles discovered in themselves a new interest in the surviving rites of religion and fostered the study of ancient literature and art. The great Hungarian scholar, Professor Alföldi, has done splendid service in tracing this Roman opposition, which he finds as early as Constantine the Great himself. It is possible that he sometimes interprets as defiance what was only intended as defence. Another focus of opposition was in the Greek schools of philosophy. They waged the lost battle until they were finally closed by Justinian in the sixth century. Last of all, but by no means least, in the heart of the country the people of the *pagi*— the pagans—retained their love of their country festivals, the worship of their gods of field and fold; they loved the old ways and were content to leave the new to the cities. The Church succeeded in ' baptising '—giving Christian

71

meaning—to much of this ancient cult. Something still was left which lingered on in the practices of witchcraft down to the border of modern times.

Of one particular point of conflict between the Church and the pagan world we happen to have a rather full account. In the senate-house of Rome stood a statue of the goddess Victory—a symbol of the invincibility of Rome— to which sacrifice was made before every meeting of the senate. This statue was removed by orders of Gratian. A few years later Symmachus, the prefect of the city, presented to Gratian's successor, Valentinian II, a formal appeal for the restoration of the statue. He pleaded that Rome should be allowed to retain those rites which she had grown hoar in honouring. Let others think her mistaken; she only asked to be left undisturbed in her error. ' But it is not possible that there should be only one way to the supreme mystery.' It was a noble and eloquent appeal; but it was successfully countered by Bishop Ambrose. The statue did not come back, except for a short period when it was replaced by the great soldier, Stilicho. But the end was not exactly what anyone had contemplated. Victory—or a figure just like her—winged and holding wreath and palm—continues on the imperial coins. True, she may now carry the cross, but her essential character cannot be mistaken. She is still Victory, but is now to be seen not as the Valkyrie of Jupiter, but as the angel of the Lord, sent to carry success to the side that He blesses. That is why the type of the Christian angel is so exactly that of the pagan goddess. Victory could still attend the arms of Rome. The cry of acclamation to the Emperor could still be: *Auguste tu vincas.*

A second similar case may be quoted. In A.D. 410 Alaric, the Visigoth, sacked Rome and exacted an enormous ransom. The Romans were driven to sore straits to raise the sum and resorted to stripping the temples of such ornaments as they still possessed. Amongst the rest they melted down the statue of the goddess whom the Romans call *Virtus.* 'And with that,' writes Zosimus, the bitter pagan who records the happening, ' finally vanished all that still was left in Rome of courage or manly worth—as the adepts in sacred lore had long foretold.' Now the figure of *Virtus* is almost indistinguishable in type from that of the goddess *Roma*. For Rome, then, she was clearly a special protectress, a *tutela*—perhaps that very mysterious power, the unnamed guardian of Rome about whom the ancients were never tired of speculating. The fatal consequences of destroying such a talisman were only too obvious to all who had eyes to see. It is rather surprising to find that the statue had survived so long; but we must consider that, as such a special talisman, it would be most jealously protected, while protection could avail. On the imperial silver coins a figure of *Virtus Romanorum* continues to take a prominent place almost down to the sack of Rome.

There are one or two more questions, too interesting to be avoided, too difficult to be answered with any confidence. We are accustomed today to apply to states analogies out of individual human life. We know of the phenomenon called conversion, sudden or gradual, in the individual. What of the same phenomenon in a state? Is conversion in this case at all comparable to that of the individual? In particular, is anything like sudden conversion possible for a state? What actually happened to Rome when Constantine changed the imperial direction?

Most of the reforms, introduced by Diocletian and Constantine, can be traced back in history; they were not so revolutionary as they at first appear. This is probably true of the reform in religion too. Steps had already been taken which made the decisive reform possible when it did come. Some steps had been taken by the State, as for instance when Gallienus granted practical toleration. Others had been taken by the Church, when she absorbed and assimilated much of the strength of Roman administration. The mere progress from obscurity and ignorance to respectability and good education made the Church a more suitable partner for the Empire. As we have seen, after Constantine there was a long interval of toleration, in which, theoretically, every man was at liberty to choose his own religious belief. Here I am stressing the gradualness of the religious change. But I do not mean to settle a very difficult question with a few apt phrases. The Christian revolution was certainly momentous in its consequences and the change is none the less because it may have been heralded by many forewarnings. I invite you to think over the problem for yourselves. Wherever Christianity has become the religion of a State, the question arises: Does this great faith stamp its mark on the State or does it not rather receive the State's mark on its own brow? Are there not points at which the State cannot be religious—so that if State and Church are not to part company, it is the Church that will have to give way? Look over the course of European history in Christian times and you will soon grant me that these questions are not irrelevant or impertinent. For Rome, the question has a particular interest as it leads on directly to another even more vital: was Christianity one of the main causes of the Decline and Fall?

Richard Garnett, in his entertaining book, *The Twilight of the Gods,* has a story of the Emperor Gallienus setting a Goth and a Christian to engage in mock combat in a little tournament which he organizes for some philosopher friends of his. The Goth swings his sword, threatening death; the Christian, unarmed, stands unafraid before him, till the Goth draws off, bitterly exclaiming that he would rather be pitted against three men in arms. Gallienus turns to his friends and observes to them: ' There you see the two men who are going to destroy Rome.' I suppose that this thought goes back to Gibbon if not earlier. It has often been echoed since. Otto Seeck, the great German historian of the late Empire, sees one of the chief causes of decline in what he calls ' Die Ausrottung der Besten ', ' The Extermination of Excellence ', and attributes it in part to the new ideas that spread with Christianity. That, of course, is less than fair; the warm humanity of Christianity does not involve any contempt for individual excellence. But we are finding today that such a noble ideal as the ' Welfare State ' may bring with it very undesirable associates—envy of those who enjoy any kind of privilege, laziness, expectation of having the best conditions with work much below the best.

Let us face the question then: Was Christianity a main cause of the decline and fall of Rome? If its coming was really a very gradual one, Rome can hardly have died of it, except in the sense that you might say a man dies by living too long. But suppose for argument's sake that its advent was more revolutionary: in that case, may Gibbon's judgement be correct?

The answer must be ' No '. The Eastern Empire was Christian, continued to be Christian and survived for centuries after the Western fell. It survived its barbarian dangers and, those once surmounted, its Christianity did not kill it. Why East Rome survived when old Rome fell is a question that will always tease students; perhaps geographical position was the decisive factor. But, as the East suffered from the same ' disease ' as the West and lived through it, the ' disease ' cannot in itself have been fatal. One might still argue that Constantinople was from the first Christian and that she therefore assimilated the new faith with a success denied to the resistant Rome. But the historical sequel does not bear this out; Rome finally bowed her head and accepted the Faith and, even when there was no more a Western Emperor, there was the Bishop of Rome —the Papacy, ' seated like a ghost in the seat of the Cæsars.'

A work of genius, written by the great Father St. Augustine, clears Christianity of any suspicion of being a power of destruction or decay. I mean ' The City of God ', written under the impression of the sack of Rome by Alaric the Visigoth, A.D. 410. The disaster shocked the world. Rome had for so long stood a sure protector against the apocalyptic terrors of the last days. Now, with the capital ravaged, who could tell how long the Empire still would stand? St. Augustine set himself to instruct Christian thought how to face the changed situation. The cities of the world, even so wonderful a city as Rome, are all imperfect, mere hints of what the true city that has foundations is, the city of God. It has always existed beside the cities of the world, obeying its own laws, the reverse of those of the world. The world pushes love of self to contempt of God; the city of God pushes love of God to contempt of self. This city cannot fall; its builder and maker is God. Whatever the unknown future, should the long familiar walls of defence collapse, the eternal city will stand. A book like this proves, if further proof be needed, that Christian thought had now a vitality capable of facing terrible changes and finding the right adjustments to them. Through the dark centuries that were to come the Christian Church maintained some bulwark against insurgent barbarism, preserved some of the treasures of ancient culture. Gibbon, great historian as he was, was debarred from really seeing Christianity by certain prejudices and half understandings in his own mind.

The study of the conflict of Church and Empire should be stimulating; for in its finer phases it was a conflict between two worthy antagonists, each with faith and energy on its side. The persecutors were wrong on the narrower point; they persecuted without sufficient cause. But they had some justification; they saw values which they honoured threatened—Roman dignity and valour, the watchful Roman peace in every province. To protect them they bitterly fought change. It proved in the end that Christianity was not one of the casual and unmeaning changes, but a logical and necessary one. The Church finally triumphed through its more abundant life; it not only outlasted its rival in the field of contest; it also outthought it, outwrote it and outlived it.

NOTES AND PASSAGES IN ILLUSTRATION

CHAPTER 1. THE ROMAN EMPIRE.

1. ROME THE TYRANT

Tacitus, *Agricola* (A.D. 98) 30 end. The Caledonian chief Calgacus speaks (A.D. 83):

'But today the boundary of Britain is exposed; beyond us lies no nation, nothing but waves and rocks and the Romans, more deadly still than they, for you find in them an arrogance which no reasonable submission can elude. Brigands of the world, they have exhausted the land by their indiscriminate plunder, and now they ransack the sea. The wealth of an enemy excites their cupidity, his poverty their lust of power. East and West have failed to glut their maw. They are unique in being as violently tempted to attack the poor as the wealthy. Robbery, butchery, rapine, the liars call Empire; they create a desolation and call it peace.'

2. ROME THE QUEEN

Rutilius, *De Reditu Suo* 47ff. A.D. 416.

'Hearken, O queen, O loveliest thing in all your realm, O Rome translated to the starry sky. Hearken, O mother of men, O mother of gods; 'tis through your temples we draw near to heaven. Of you we sing and will sing while fate allows; no man can be alive—forgetting you. . . . Far abroad as human life extends, every land has made way for your valour to pass. For sundered nations you have made one fatherland; under your rule the sinners have only gained by their defeat. You offer to your defeated foes the partnership in your rights; you have made one city of what was once a world.'

3. A MODERN ESTIMATE

Gibbon, *Decline and Fall of the Roman Empire.* Vol I. Chap. 3, near end.

'If a man were called to fix the period in the history of the world during which the condition of the human race was most happy and prosperous, he would without hesitation name that which elapsed from the death of Domitian to the accession of Commodus (A.D. 96-180). The vast extent of the Roman empire was governed by absolute power, under the guidance of virtue and wisdom. The armies were restrained by the firm but gentle hand of four successive emperors, whose characters and authority commanded involuntary respect. . . . Such princes deserved the honour of restoring the republic, had the Romans of their days been capable of enjoying a rational freedom.'

CHAPTER 2. THE RELIGIONS OF THE ROMAN EMPIRE

1. FORMS OF ROMAN RELIGION

Acta Ludorum Saecularium. 17 B.C. Part of the night prayer to the Fates.

Augustus prays: ' Ye Fates, even as it is written in the sacred Books, even so to the advantage of the Roman people the Quirites be this sacrifice made to you: I beg and beseech you that ye magnify the empire and majesty of the Roman people the Quirites in war and peace, and that ye ever protect the Latin name, that ye give eternal surety victory and health to the Roman people aforesaid, that ye bless the Roman people aforesaid and the legions of that same Roman people, and that ye keep the estate of the Roman people aforesaid safe from all harms, and that ye be kind and favourable to the Roman people aforesaid, to the college of the fifteen priests, to me, to my house and family and that ye graciously receive this sacrifice of nine ewe-lambs and nine she-goats. . . .'

2. WORSHIP OF ISIS

Apuleius, *The Golden Ass* (translated by Robert Graves, Penguin Classics). Chaps. XVII and XVIII. The goddess Isis appears in answer to the prayer of the enchanted ass:

' You see me here, Lucius, in answer to your prayer. I am Nature, the universal Mother, mistress of all the elements, primordial child of time, sovereign of all things spiritual, queen of the dead, queen also of the immortals, the single manifestation of all gods and goddesses that are. My nod governs the shining heights of Heaven, the wholesome sea-breezes, the lamentable silences of the world below! '

All races worship her under different names—Mother of the Gods, Artemis, Aphrodite, Dictynna, Proserpina. Only the Egyptians know her by her true name, Isis. Lucius is now to be restored to human shape at her festival of the sea, and then:

' It is only right that you should devote your whole life to the Goddess who makes you a man again. Under my protection you will be happy and famous, and when at the destined end of your life you descend to the land of ghosts, there too in the subterrene hemisphere you shall have frequent occasion to adore me. From the Elysian fields you will see me as queen of the profound Stygian realm, shining through the darkness of Acheron with a light as kindly and tender as I show you now. Further, if you are found to deserve my divine protection by careful obedience to the ordinances of my religion and by perfect chastity, you will become aware that I, and I alone, have power to prolong your life beyond the limits appointed by destiny.'

Lucius then received back his human shape and became an initiate of the goddess. He cannot give away the secrets of this rite but

'I will record as much as I may lawfully record for the uninitiated, but only on condition that you believe it. I approached the very gates of death and set foot on Proserpina's threshold, yet was permitted to return, rapt through all the elements. At midnight I saw the sun shining as if it were noon; I entered the presence of the gods of the underworld and the gods of the upper world, stood near and worshipped them.'

3. STOICISM

Lucan, *Pharsalia*. IX. 564ff.

As they pass the temple of Ammon in the Libyan desert, Labienus begs Cato to consult the oracle. 'What shall I ask?' says Cato, 'Whether a freeman's death is better than a slave's life? Whether virtue is the supreme good?' He knows the answers; Ammon can add nothing. He goes on:

'To heaven we all are tied; in temple still
Nothing we do that is not by God's will.
God needs no utterance, who instilled at birth
Whatever we may rightly know on earth.
Or, that his voice only by few be heard,
Chose he this desert, here the truth interred?
In earth and sea and sky the godhead dwells,
In heaven, in virtue. What then seek we else?
All that your eyes can see, all that can stir
Within your human heart is Jupiter.'

4. EPICUREANISM

Lucretius, *De Rerum Natura* III. 18ff. (Translation by Cyril Bailey, 1947.)

'The majesty of the gods is revealed and their peaceful abodes, which neither the winds shake nor clouds soak with showers, nor does the snow congealed with biting frost besmirch them with its white fall, but an ever cloudless sky vaults them over, and smiles with light bounteously spread around. Moreover, nature supplies all they need, nor does anything gnaw at their peace of mind at any time.'

Ibid. I. 44ff.

'For it must needs be that all the nature of the gods enjoys life everlasting in perfect peace, sundered and separated far away from our world. For free from all grief, free from danger, mighty in its own resources, never lacking aught of us, it is not won by virtuous service nor touched by wrath.'

5. Emperor Worship

Athenaeus, *Deipnosophistae*. VI. 253. Hymn (sung at Athens) to Demetrius Poliorcetes:

> 'Son of Posidon, mighty god, and Aphrodite, hail!
> For other gods are far away; or does their hearing fail?
> They don't exist or don't attend to us for any good,
> But you we see, not wood or stone, but present, flesh
>   and blood.'

And so they pray to him.

Lucan, *Pharsalia*. I. 44ff. Dedication to Nero.

Yet Rome owes much to the civil war—because it gave her Nero. When at some far day he returns to Heaven—to hold the sceptre of Jupiter or drive the chariot of the Sun—he has only to choose—let him be careful not to place himself either due North or due South. He might upset the balance of the universe. However that be, the human race may then lay aside its arms and consult its true interests; the nations may love one another and peace reign. Nero will inspire Lucan better than could Apollo or Bacchus; he is the right inspiration for a Roman song.

Martial, *Ep*. VIII. 21. Written for the return of Domitian to Rome:

> 'O star of morning, bring us back the day;
> Cæsar is coming, why our joys delay?
> O bring us back the day.'

Some frigid conceits follow about the slowness of the Wain of the Great Bear which the star must be taking and the steed of Castor which he ought to borrow for the occasion. The Sun with his horses is ready; the Dawn is awake. Yes, but the stars decline to give place and the Moon insists on seeing the Emperor come.

> 'Come then, O Cæsar, e'n though it be by night;
> Let the stars keep their stations for the sight;
> Come and your people shall not want for light.'

CHAPTER 3. THE CHURCH AND THE EMPIRE DOWN TO TRAJAN.

1. Persecution in the New Testament

I have referred occasionally to what the New Testament tells us of relations with the Roman government. It may be valuable to look a little more closely at what is said of persecution in the New Testament. Persecution in *Acts* and the *Epistles* of St. Paul comes from the Jews, not as a rule from the Romans. Perhaps just because he was a Roman citizen St. Paul takes an optimistic view of what the authorities will do. The Synoptic Gospels add persecution by the government to that by the Jews. Christians will not only be persecuted in the synagogues; they will be brought unto magistrates, before kings and rulers; they will be persecuted, says Jesus, ' for My name's sake '. In all three synoptic Gospels persecution comes into the accounts of the coming disaster to Jerusalem. All three, then, know of the persecution under Nero. The fourth Gospel has different emphases. ' In the world ye shall have tribulation '—the Christian life is one of battle; but persecution is not one of the things that interest St. John most. The first Epistle of St. Peter is most explicit. It is written from Babylon (surely the spiritual Babylon, Rome). Its readers have to suffer a fiery trial; the Gentiles speak evil of them as evil-doers; they must suffer not as malefactors, but as Christians, and bear reproach for the name. The duty of submission to lawful authority is still emphasized. Second Peter adds little and, as its date is disputed, I will not dwell on it here. It is the Apocalypse, of course, that gives us the most lurid picture of persecution. The seat of Satan at Pergamum; the Seven Churches, all being sorely tried and sustaining their trial with various degrees of fortitude; the souls of the victims under the altar; those that came out of great tribulation and washed their robes and made them white in the blood of the Lamb; the Beast and his number; the woman drunk with the blood of the Saints; the fall of Babylon the Great—all tell of a time of suffering and bitterness and speak not of measured resentment of wrongs, but of burning hatred of Rome and its Emperors.

2. PLUTARCH OF CHAERONEA, first to second century A.D. Great biographer, essayist, etc.

Plutarch, *On Superstition*. Chap. 1. Lack of study and knowledge about the gods leads on the one hand to atheism, in ' tough ' minds, on the other to superstition in ' tender '.

Chap. 2. . . . ' Now atheism, being a false judgement denying the existence of the blessed and incorruptible, seems, through its distrust of the divine, to lead to a kind of insensibility; superstition (fear of the gods) is declared by its very name to be an impassioned belief, a terrifying conception of something that humbles and depresses man, when he conceives that gods exist, but that they are unkind and hurtful.'

Chap. 4 The fears of the superstitious extend beyond life. ' The gates of Hell yawn below, rivers of fire, Styx and his tributaries roll, the darkness is full of ghosts, hard-faced, sad-voiced, there are judges, torturers, gulfs and dens full of horrors without end.'

Chap. 8. 'God is the hope of courage, not the excuse of cowardice.' (The example of the Jews butchered unresisting on their Sabbath is hardly just.)

Chap. 12. Superstition begets atheism. Atheism would stand chidden before the order and majesty of the universe but 'superstition with its ridiculous behaviours and feelings, its incantations, enchantments, magic rites, processions, beatings of drums, unclean purifications and filthy cleansings, the barbarous and unnatural punishments and indignities that accompany its services—this, I assert, makes some men say that, if the gods are like that, fond of such offerings and delights, brutal, petty, vindictive, it is better that they should not exist at all'.

Chap. 14. Plutarch concludes: 'So some men, running away from superstition, fall into the hard and repellent pit of atheism, jumping over religion which lies between the two'

3. *RELIGIO* AND *SUPERSTITIO*.

Tacitus and Pliny both call Christianity a *superstitio,* 'horrible' or 'evil and immoderate'. This raises a question, not of religious creed or form, but of religious instinct and feeling; what is *superstitio* and how does it differ from religion?

The Roman people ranked as very religious, very anxious to preserve the 'peace', the right relationship with the gods. Polybius, the Greek historian, saw much superstition in Roman state religion, but strongly approved of it, because it kept the masses in order. Lucretius, the impassioned Epicurean, thought all that is usually called religion no better than superstition. Epicurus, setting men free from religion,

'From stormy waves, from such abyss of night
Brought life to such a calm, so clear a light.'

The Augustan age brought a revival of religion. Augustus rebuilt the temples and encouraged the good old Roman *mores*. His poets, Virgil and Horace, seconded his efforts in their poetry. It is religion, not superstition, that is here in question, even if Augustus had some funny little personal superstitions.

Seneca, Stoic philosopher, imperial tutor, minister of State—and multi-millionaire,—in his lost *De superstitione* derided many features of Roman religion; but, as St. Augustine says, he wrote more courageously than he lived. Seneca makes no mention of the Christians for good or bad—not to offend Roman prejudice and not to go against his own judgement, maybe, by blaming them.

Tacitus and Pliny were both, we should gather, conventional observers of religious forms. Tacitus, not Pliny, lets us know, here and there, that he forms his own theories about the gods and their conduct. They are concerned not to protect, but to punish. They are indifferent to human virtue or vice.

Why then is Christianity called a 'superstition'?. Tacitus may have had in mind the supposed crimes of Christians; but, after his governorship in Asia just after Pliny in Bithynia, he should have known better. And what of Pliny? What is there superstitious in the practices of the Christians as he detected them? What could there be to deserve so harsh a name—unless it were the hymn sung to Christ as God?

4. A ROMAN HYMN.
Horace, *Carmen Saeculare*. 17 B.C.

> Phoebus and Dian woodland queen,
> Worshipful still, as worshipped ye have been,
> Bright lights of heaven, grant the prayer we pray
> > This holy day

> Whereon Sibylline verses bade
> Each holy boy and each elected maid
> To hymn the gods whose loving presence fills
> > The Seven Hills.

> Warm Sun who in your car of flame
> Bring day and hide it, ever born the same
> Yet other, come there nothing to your sight
> > Than Rome more bright.

> Looser, Light-bringer, Queen of Birth—
> Whatever name you choose to show your worth—
> The mothers in due season bless for whom
> > You ope the womb.

> > . . .

> May Earth, fecund of crops and kind,
> Round Ceres's head the wreath of corn-ears bind;
> May breeze of heaven and healthful water's flow
> > Bless all that grow.

> > . . .

> Faith, Peace, Renown, antique Respect
> And Valour venture back from long neglect
> And with her horn, full of the happy years,
> > Plenty appears.

> The prophet, darling of the Nine,
> Who radiant with bow of gold doth shine,
> Phoebus, who heals our weariness and smart
> > With gentle art,

Our sacrifices here commends
And to glad Latium and Rome extends
New term of life and blessings ever growing
    To overflowing.

She who on Aventine doth reign
And Algidus, Diana, hears the strain
The priests incant and bends a kindly brow
    On children's vow.

Jove and the gods share this concern;
With this good hope and sure we home return,
To Phoebus and Diana taught to raise
    Our choir of praise.

CHAPTER 4. THE CHURCH AND THE EMPIRE: HADRIAN TO TRAJAN DECIUS AND VALERIAN.

1. RESCRIPT OF HADRIAN.

Eusebius, *Ecclesiastical History*. IV. 9. (Translation by Kirsopp Lake, Loeb.)

'To Minucius Fundanus. I received a letter written to me from his Excellency, Serennius Granianus, your predecessor. I think that the matter ought not to remain without inquiry, to prevent men from being harassed or helping the rascality of informers. If then the provincials can make out a case on these lines against the Christians so as to plead it in open court, let them be influenced by this alone and not by opinions or mere outcries. For it is far more correct if anyone wishes to make an accusation for you to examine this point. If then anyone accuses them and shows that they are acting illegally, decide the point according to the nature of the offence, but by Hercules, if anyone brings the matter forward for the purpose of blackmail, investigate strenuously and be careful to inflict penalties adequate to the crime.'

2. A 'LIBELLUS' OF THE DECIAN PERSECUTION.

'To the officers in charge of the sacrifices of the village of Alexander's Isle, from Aurelius Diogenes, the son of Satabus, from the village of Alexander's Isle, aged about 72, with a scar on his right eyebrow. I have always sacrificed to the gods; and now in your presence, according to the commands, I have sacrificed and made a libation and tasted of the victims; and I desire you to subscribe. Fare ye well.'

'I, Aurelius Diogenes, have delivered this . . .'

'I, Mys . . . (saw him) sacrificing and have subscribed.
In the first year of Imperator Cæsar Gaius Messius Quintus Traianus Decius Pius Felix Augustus, on Epiphi 2.' (June 26, 250).

3. ORIGINES, *Contra Celsum*. I. 68.

'In the next place Celsus, suspecting that we shall put forward the mighty works of Jesus, of which we have already spoken very slightly, professes to grant that they may be true—all that is recorded of healings, or of a resurrection, or of the many who fed on a few loaves and left of them many fragments, and all the rest of the stories in telling which he thinks the disciples were romancing—and adds, ' Well, suppose we believe that you really did them.' Then straightway he puts them on a level with the works of the jugglers, on the ground that their professions are still more marvellous, and with the performances of the Egyptians, who sell their venerated arts for a few pence in the open market-place, and cast out demons from men, and puff away diseases, and call up souls of heroes, and exhibit costly dinners with tables and cakes and dainties non-existent, and set in motion as living animals lifeless things which have only the appearance of animals. Then he says, ' Since the jugglers do these things, must we needs think them sons of God, or shall we say that these are practices of wicked wretches? '

4. SELECTIONS FROM TERTULLIAN. *Apologeticus* (Translation by Glover, Loeb.)

I. 7. ' Men proclaim aloud that the state is beset with us; in countryside, in village, in islands, Christians; every sex, age, condition, yes! and rank going over to the name.'

II. 3. ' But to Christians alone it is forbidden to say anything to clear their case, to defend truth, to save the judge from being unjust. No! one thing is looked for, one alone, the one thing needed for popular hatred—the confession of the name. Not investigation of the charge.'

II. 7. The inconsistency of Trajan. ' He says they must not be sought out, implying that they are innocent; and he orders them to be punished, implying they are guilty. He spares them and rages against them, he pretends not to see and punishes.'

II. 10. ' The Christians alone you torture to make them deny.'

IV. 4. ' When you harshly cut the case short by saying ' your existence is illegal ' . . . your dictum means force, an unjust tyranny from the citadel.'

X. 1ff. The gods were once men.

XVII. 6. Men naturally speak of God, not of gods. ' O the witness of the soul, in its very nature Christian '.

XXI. 1ff. ' Perhaps some question may be raised as to the standing of the school on the ground that, under cover of a very famous religion (and one certainly permitted by law), the school insinuates quietly certain claims of its own.'

XXI. 24. 'The whole story of Christ was reported to Cæsar . . . by Pilate, himself in his secret heart already a Christian.'

XXIV. 6. 'Look to it, whether this also may form part of the accusation of irreligion—to do away with freedom of religion, to forbid a man choice of deity, so that I may not worship whom I would, but am forced to worship whom I would not.'

XXVIII. 2. 'So now we have come to the second charge, the charge of treason against a majesty more august. For it is with fear and shrewder timidity that you watch Cæsar, than Olympian Jove himself. . . . In fact among you perjury by all the gods together comes quicker than by the genius of a single Cæsar.'

XXX. 4. 'We pray for them (the Emperors) long life, a secure rule, a safe home, brave armies, a faithful senate, an honest people, a quiet world—and everything for which a man and a Cæsar can pray.'

XXXII. 1. 'We know that the great force which threatens the whole estate of the empire and the end of the age itself with its menace of hideous suffering is delayed by the respite which the Roman empire means for us.'

XXXIV. 4. 'It is a curse before his apotheosis to call Cæsar god.'

XXXV. 7. 'Jupiter take our years to add to thine.' A Christian can no more utter these words than wish for a new Cæsar.

XXXVII. 4f. 'We are but of yesterday, and we have filled everything you have—cities, islands, forts, towns, exchanges, yes! and camps, tribes, decuries, palace, senate, forum. All we have left you is the temples.' A mere secession would put the Roman world to the blush. 'Nearly all the citizens you have in nearly all the cities are Christians' . . . 'But you have preferred to call us enemies of the human race rather than of human error.'

XXXVIII. 1. . . . 'Was not a rather gentler treatment in order? Should not this school have been classed among tolerated associations, when it commits no such actions as are commonly feared from unlawful associations?'

XXXIX. 7. '"Look," they say, "how they love one another" (for they themselves hate one another) "and how they are ready to die for one another". But even that is made a charge against the Christians.'

XL. 12. 'If the Tiber reaches the walls, if the Nile does not rise to the fields, if the sky doesn't move or the earth does, if there is famine, if there is plague, the cry is heard at once: " The Christians to the lion." What, all of them to one lion?'

XL. 15. The prayers of Christians win God's mercy; 'and then, when we have wrung mercy from Him,—Jupiter has all the glory.'

XLVI. 2ff. Perhaps we are only a new philosophy. But you don't persecute philosophers. 'They openly destroy your gods, they attack your superstitions in their treatises, and you applaud. Yes, and many of them bark against your Emperors too, and you sustain them. You are more ready to reward them with statues and stipends than to condemn them to the beasts. Quite right too! Philosophers is what they are called, not Christians. The name of philosopher does not drive out demons.'

XLVIII. 10. ' " Then," do you ask, " will it always be dying and rising again? " If the Lord of all things had so determined you would have perforce to submit to the law that governed your being.'

L. 12ff. Yes, you magistrates, you may please the mobs by your cruelties to us but you waste your pains. 'We multiply whenever we are mown down by you; the blood of Christians is seed. . . . There is a rivalry between God's ways and man's; we are condemned by you, we are acquitted by God.'

TERTULLIAN, *de Spectaculis*

XXIX. The Christian has his own pleasures to make up for those of the public shows. 'Have you a mind for blood? You have the blood of Christ.'

XXX. After a terrible passage about the punishment of the wicked in hell, Tertullian ends on a happier note, the eternal joys of the faithful. 'But what are those things which eye hath not seen nor ear heard, nor ever entered into the heart of man? I believe things of greater joy than circus, theatre or amphitheatre, or any stadium.'

5. LUCIAN, *The Death of Peregrine.* (Translation by H. W. and F. G. Fowler, Oxford, 1905.)

Peregrine, or Proteus, as he liked to be called, has burned himself on a pyre at Olympia. Just before this happened, a man in the crowd gave some details of Peregrine's former life:

' It was now that he came across the priests and scribes of the Christians in Palestine, and picked up their queer creed.' He got on fast and in the end was arrested and imprisoned. 'The Christians took it all very seriously; he was no sooner in prison than they began trying every means to get him out again

—but without success. . . . Orphans and ancient widows might be seen hanging about the prison from break of day. . . . Elegant dinners were conveyed in; their sacred writings were read.' Some churches in Asia sent deputations with offers of sympathy, assistance and legal advice. So Peregrine did very well. 'You see, these misguided creatures start with the general conviction that they are immortal for all time, which explains the contempt of death and voluntary self-devotion which are so common among them; and then it was impressed on them by their original lawgiver that they are all brothers, from the moment that they are converted, and deny the gods of Greece, and worship the crucified sage, and live after his laws. All this they take quite on trust, with the result that they despise all worldly goods alike, regarding them merely as common property. Now an adroit, unscrupulous fellow, who has seen the world, has only to get among these simple soûls, and his fortune is pretty soon made; he plays with them.'

CHAPTER 5. THE CHURCH AND THE EMPIRE: GALLIENUS TO CONSTANTINE THE GREAT.

1. JUPITER AND HERCULES

(a) Arnobius, *Against the Heathen*. I. 38.

'But supposing that we give in for a moment to your views and admit that Christ was one of us, with the same mind, soul, body and frail condition as ours, is He not worthy to be called God, to be felt as God by us in view of our gratitude for all His gifts? For if you have given a place in Heaven to Liber because he discovered the use of wine, to Ceres because she discovered bread, to Aesculapius for healing herbs, to Minerva for oil, to Triptolemus for the plough, above all to Hercules, because he quelled wild beasts, thieves and many-headed water-snakes, what honours ought not we to pay Him who sent His truth into our hearts and reclaimed us from our dire errors?'

I. 40. The heathen mock at Christians for worshipping One who died a shameful death. 'But have you not adopted as guardian and patron of health and salvation that Aesculapius, who, after discovering medicines, was punished by the thunderbolt? Do you not invite as guest with sacrifices, victims and burning of incense that very mighty Hercules, who by your own account was smitten by affliction, burnt alive and reduced to ashes on the fatal pyre?' . . .

(b) *Panegyric (incerti auctoris)*. XI. 14. (A.D. 289.) The panegyrist assures the Emperor Maximian that, wherever he may seek retirement, all lands and seas are full of him. The world, 'full of Jupiter', is also 'full of Hercules'.

2. THE VISION OF CONSTANTINE

The account of Eusebius (*Life of Constantine I*. 28, 29) is as follows: the Emperor, when in Gaul with his army, saw above the setting sun the sign of the Cross, outlined in rays of light, and with it the words *Hoc signo victor eris*. Christ in a dream explained to Constantine what it meant. The Emperor then caused the *labarum,* the imperial standard, to be made and wore the initial letters of the name of the Redeemer on his helmet.

The account of Lactantius, *De Mortibus Persecutorum*, 44.5.6, is different. The Vision was in a dream before the battle of the Mulvian Bridge and what Constantine saw was not the Cross, but the sacred initials XP, in the form ☧

3. DECREE OF TOLERATION ISSUED BY THE EMPERORS, GALERIUS, CONSTANTINE AND LICINIUS

'Among the many plans that we have had in mind for the public good and weal, we have hitherto designed to direct all things according to the ancient laws and general principles of the Romans and so to provide that the Christians—who indeed have abandoned the choice of their own ancestors,—may return to a sound state of mind. But something or other has led them to be possessed by such a presumption, obsessed by such a folly that they cannot follow the precepts laid down of old—precepts which their own fathers maybe established,—but according to their own choice and the will of each must make their own code of laws and keep them and collect their several congregations in sundry places; and so, when an edict went out from us that they should adapt themselves to that which the ancients have ordained, very many of them became subject to peril, very many were troubled and like to die by many a death; and, whereas, with the greater part of them abiding in their desperate folly, we saw that they were neither giving the service due to the gods of heaven nor devoting themselves to their own Christian worship, we in our love for men and our constant practice of extending our forgiveness to all have now most readily chosen so to deal with this trouble too and so far to extend our indulgence as to permit Christians again to exist and to restore the houses in which they meet—providing that they do nothing contrary to discipline; in another letter we will make clear to our judges what principle they will have to observe. So now after this our indulgence it is their duty to beseech their God for our salvation, that of the State and of themselves, that so in every way public affairs may be preserved safe and sound and that they may be able to live free from care at their own hearths.'

4. THE FATE OF THE PERSECUTORS

Lactantius, *De Mortibus Persecutorum*.

I. . . . 'For God has raised up princes who have made void the wicked and cruel commands of the tyrants and have wisely cared for the human race, so that the clouds of the past are dispersed and joyous and serene light gladdens the hearts of all. . . . See, the conspiracy of evil men has been quenched and God wipes away the tears from the mourners' eyes; those who had overthrown the holy temple have fallen in heavier ruin themselves; those who butchered the just have breathed out their guilty souls under torments well merited—all too late indeed, but bitter and their desert.'

IX. Galerius, the worst of the bad. 'He had the natural savagery of a wild animal and a ferocity unnatural to Roman blood. But no wonder, for his mother, a native of Dacia over the Danube, had crossed before the attacks of the Carpi to new Dacia. His body matched his character; he was tall, his body was spread and bloated to a horrible size. In word, action, aspect he scared and intimidated everybody. His father-in-law even was desperately afraid of him. . . .'

XI. 'And since Diocletian could not fight against his friends and his Cæsar and Apollo, he still tried to be moderate so far as to require the persecution to stop short of blood; the Cæsar would have had all who objected to sacrifice burned alive.'

XXXI. 'From him (Maximian Herculius) God, the avenger of his religion and his people, now turned his eyes to the other Maximian, the author of the wicked persecution, that on him too he might prove the might of his vengeance. . . . It was in his eighteenth year that God smote him with a blow past cure. A malignant ulcer started in his groin and began to spread. The surgeons operated and tried to heal it. When a scab had formed the wound broke out again, and, a vein being severed, there was a hemorrhage that was almost fatal. And soon the wound began to resist treatment; it invaded the rear part of the body and, the more it was cut back, it raged the wilder. . . .' He was eaten by worms. Then at last he repented and issued his edict of toleration.

LII. 'Where are now those glorious names, once famed among the peoples, of the Jovii and Herculiani—first insolently adopted by Diocletian and Maximian and handed on from them to their successors? How cheap have they become! Yes, God has blotted them out, removed their trace from the earth. Let us celebrate the triumph of our God with exultation, the victory of the Lord with praise in prayers by day and prayers by night; let us praise Him that, having after those ten years given His people peace, He may confirm that peace for ever.'

5. JUDGEMENT ON CONSTANTINE

Gibbon, *Decline and Fall of the Roman Empire*. Chap. XX.

' Instead of asserting his just superiority above the imperfect heroism and profane philosophy of Trajan and the Antonines, the mature age of Constantine forfeited the reputation which he had acquired in his youth. As he gradually advanced in the knowledge of truth, he proportionally declined in the practice of virtue; and the same year of his reign in which he convened the council of Nice was polluted by the execution, or rather murder, of his eldest son. . . . At the time of the death of Crispus, the Emperor could no longer hesitate in the choice of religion; he could no longer be ignorant that the Church was possessed of an infallible remedy, though he chose to defer the application of it, till the approach of death had removed the temptation and danger of a relapse.'

6. CONSTANTINE THE GREAT. *Letter to the Bishops of Arles.*

' The incomprehensible kindness of our God by no means allows the state of man to stray for too long a time in the darkness. Nor does it suffer the odious wills of some so to prevail as not to grant men a new opportunity for conversion to the truth by opening up before them through its most glorious light a path to salvation. Of this indeed I am assured by many examples and I can illustrate the same truth from my own case. For at the first there were in me things which appeared far removed from righteousness and I did not think that there was any heavenly power which could see into the secrets of my heart. What fortune ought these things which I have mentioned to have brought upon me?—surely one overflowing with every evil. But Almighty God, who sitteth in the watch-tower of Heaven, has bestowed upon me that which I did not deserve, and truly, most holy bishops of the Saviour Christ, at this time I can neither describe nor number these gifts which of His heavenly benevolence He has granted to me, His servant.'

' When godlessness, far and wide, lay heavy upon men, when the State was threatened by the deadly pestilence of utter corruption and a radical cure was the urgent need, what a relief, what a salvation from the mischief did God contrive! . . . God decreed my service and accounted me fit to execute His decree. And thus have I, setting out from the sea in Britain and the lands where the sun must set, driven out and scattered the terrors that ruled on every hand by power from on High; that mankind, instructed by my mission, might return to the service of the Holy Law and that our most blessed Faith might also be spread abroad, under the mighty direction of the Highest.

Being convinced that this was my glorious task, this God's gracious gift to me, I come now also to the lands of the East, which, in their bitter pains, require my earnest aid.'

'What each man out of conviction undertakes himself, he shall not try to force on another. What a man sees and realizes for himself, let him serve his neighbour therewith, if he may; but if he avails not so to do, let him leave it alone. For it is one thing to undertake of one's own free will the battle for the hereafter, another to compel men by punishment to do so. I have stated this and explained it more fully than my grace intended as I would not conceal my Christian faith. I have done so because, I am told, some men are saying that the usages of the pagan temples have been abolished together with the powers of pagan darkness. Indeed, I would so counsel every man, were it not that the rebellious might of false doctrines, to the injury of the salvation of us all, has struck its roots so terribly deep.'

CHAPTER 6.   THE CHRISTIAN EMPIRE.

1. WAR ON PAGANISM

Firmicus Maternus, *De Errore Profanarum Religionum*. c. A.D. 350.

Chap. XXI. 'To you, O Constantius and Constans, most sacred Emperors, must I now appeal—to you and to the might of your revered faith, which rises above our human level, withdraws from earthly frailty and joins the company of heaven, which, in its every act, serves to the best of its powers the will of God. Only a little remains to do ere the devil lies in utter ruin before your laws, ere the deadly contagion of a dead idolatry ceases to be. The venom of the poison has grown weak; day by day the reality of its profane desires declines. Raise high the standard of the Faith. Blessed are ye whom God has chosen to be sharers in His glory and His will, blessed ye for whose hands Christ in His favour has reserved the destruction of idolatry, the overthrow of the heathen temples.'

Chap. XXIX. 'Most sacred Emperors, strip the temples of their ornaments, strip and fear not. Let those vain gods be melted down by the fire of the mint or the blaze of the metal-worker's flame. Transfer all the temple gifts to the use of yourselves and of the Lord. Since you destroyed the temples, you have advanced mightily by the strong help of God. . . . It only remains to destroy the forbidden idols.'

2. JULIAN THE APOSTATE

(a) The Emperors are tried out on their merits before an assembly of the gods. *Caesares* 335, 336.

Marcus Aurelius gains the reward. The rest choose their own guardians and guides. Alexander hastened to Hercules, Octavian to Apollo and so on. Constantine could not discover among the gods the model of his own career, but when he caught sight of Luxury who was not far off, he ran to her. . . . There too he found Jesus, who had taken up his abode with her and cried aloud to all comers: ' He that is a seducer, he that is a murderer, he that is sacrilegious and infamous, let him approach without fear! For with this water will I wash him and will straightway make him clean. And though he should be guilty of those same sins a second time, let him but smite his breast and beat his head and I will make him clean again.'

(b) *Letter to a Priest*, 305 B.

' Even though he be poor and a man of the people, if he possess within himself these two things, love for God and love for his fellow men, let him be appointed priest '. . . . ' We must pay especial attention to this point and by this means effect a cure. For when it came about that the poor were neglected and overlooked by the priests, then I think the impious Galilaeans observed this fact and devoted themselves to philanthropy.' It is like bribing children with cakes. So with their love-feasts, and hospitality, and service of tables, they have led very many into atheism.

3. THE VERDICT OF GIBBON

Gibbon, *Decline and Fall of the Roman Empire*. Chap. XV ff.

It is hard to isolate in any one or two passages that peculiar irony which Gibbon has thought fit to expend on the Christian Faith. I select one or two which give the general tone.

Chap. XVI. ' In this general view of the persecution, which was first authorized by the edicts of Diocletian, I have purposely refrained from describing the particular sufferings and deaths of the Christian martyrs. . . . These melancholy scenes might be enlivened by a crowd of visions and miracles, destined either to delay the death, to celebrate the triumph, or to discover the relics of those canonized saints who suffered for the name of Christ. But I cannot determine what I ought to transcribe, till I am satisfied how much I ought to believe. . . . We shall conclude this chapter by a melancholy truth, which obtrudes itself on the reluctant mind; that even admitting, without hesitation or inquiry, all that history has recorded or devotion has feigned, on the subject of martyrdoms, it must still be acknowledged that the Christians, in the course of their intestine dissensions, have inflicted far greater severities on each other, than they had experienced from the zeal of infidels. . . . A people elated by pride, or soured by discontent, are seldom qualified to form a just estimate of their actual situation. The subjects of Constantine were incapable of discerning the decline of genius and manly virtue, which so far degraded them below the dignity of their ancestors; but they could feel and lament the rage of tyranny, the relaxation of discipline, and the increase of taxes. . . . The rights of mankind might derive some protection from religion and philosophy; and the name of freedom, which could no longer alarm, might sometimes admonish, the successors of Augustus, that they did not reign over a nation of slaves or barbarians.'

'The triumph of barbarism and religion.'

'From these innocent barbarians the reproach may be transferred to the Catholics of Rome.'

4. THE CITY OF GOD

St. Augustine, *The City of God* (F. A. Wright's Selection).

II. 20. 'Let the poor cringe to the rich for the sake of a full stomach, that under their patronage they may enjoy a sluggish tranquillity. Let the rich misuse the help of the poor to make them their dependants and to minister to their pride. Let the people applaud, not those who consult their true interests, but those who provide them lavishly with pleasures. Let no stern duty be commanded, no filthiness forbidden. Let it be a ruler's object to secure, not the loyalty, but the servility of his subjects. Let the provinces render obedience to their rulers, not as being their moral guides, but as being their worldly masters and the purveyors of their pleasures; and let them feel not an honest respect but a slavish fear. . . . Let those be reckoned the true gods, who procure this happiness for the people and assure them this enjoyment. Let them be worshipped as they wish; let them demand whatever games they wish, to be observed in the company or at the expense of their worshippers; only let them see to it that this happiness has nothing to fear from enemies, pestilence, or disaster of any kind.'

IV. 4. 'And so, if you take away justice, what are kingdoms but brigandage on the grand scale? And what is brigandage but royalty on the small?'

IV. 17. 'But maybe they say that Jupiter sends the goddess, Victory, and that she, obedient to the king of the gods, passes to that side that he has chosen and there abides. This in truth applies not to that Jupiter whom they in their fond imagination make out to be the king of the gods, but to the true King of the Ages; for he sends, not Victory, who has no actual existence, but His angel and makes the side he wills victorious.'

V. 26. 'Soldiers who were in the battle (of the Frigidus) have told me that the spears that they tried to throw were wrenched from their hands—the wind blowing furiously from the side of Theodosius against his enemies and not only hurling on forcibly all that was aimed at them, but even twisting round their own weapons on themselves.'

XI. 1. 'We have learned that there is a City of God, in which we have desired to be citizens from that love which its founder has inspired in us. . . . (Augustine has devoted ten books to describing the enemies of the holy City.) . . . 'Now to the best of my powers I will try to give an account of the beginnings, the ends and the defining limits of these two cities, the earthly and the heavenly, which, as we have said, are, in this our intermediate age, in some sense confounded and entangled one with the other.'

XIV. 28. 'And so two cities have been created by two loves; the earthly city by love of self even to contempt of God, the heavenly city by love of God even to contempt of self. The one city glories in itself; the other glories in the Lord. The one seeks glory from men; the other finds its greatest glory in God the witness of conscience. The one lifts its head in its own glory; the other says to its God, ' Thou art my glory, Thou dost lift up my head.' In the one, among its princes, and the nations it subdues, the love of dominion holds sway; in the other princes and subjects serve one another in love, the former by wise counsel, the latter by obedience. The one loves its own strength as shown in the persons of its rulers; the other says to its God, 'I will love Thee, O Lord, my strength.' In the earthly city the wise have always lived by men's rules. But in the other city there is no human wisdom save piety, whereby the true God is duly worshipped, and it looks for its reward in the society of holy men and holy angels, ' that God may be all in all.'

LIST OF RECOMMENDED BOOKS

The following is a select list of books recommended to be read in conjunction with these lectures:—

Alföldi, A.: *Conversion of Constantine and Pagan Rome* (1948).

Angus, S.: *The Religious Quests of the Graeco-Roman World* (1929).

Bible, New Testament: *Apocryphal New Testament,* tr. James (1924).

Bigg, C.: *The Church's Task under the Roman Empire* (1905).

Bigg, C.: *The Origins of Christianity* (1909).

Charlesworth, M. P.: *The Roman Empire* (1951).

Deissmann, A.: *Light from the Ancient East* (1910).

Duchesne, L.: *Early History of the Christian Church.* 3 vols. (1950-51).

Frend, W. H. C.: *The Donatist Church* (1952).

Gwatkin, H. M.: *Early Church History to A.D. 313.* 2 vols. (1909).

Gwatkin, H. M.: *Selections from Early Christian Writers* (1897).

Harnack, A.: *History of Dogma.* 7 vols. (1896-99).

Lietzmann, H.: *The Beginnings of the Christian Church* (1937).

Lietzmann, H.: *The Founding of the Church Universal* (1938).

Nock, A. D.: *Conversion* (1933).

Ramsay, Sir W. M.: *The Church in the Roman Empire* (1893).

Rostovtsev, M. J.: *History of the Ancient World.* Vol 2: *Rome* (1928).

PLATES

PLATE I

1. Bronze Medallion, *c*. A.D. 330. Urbs Roma: She-wolf and Twins (pp. 11, 77).

2. Sestertius of Hadrian, *c*. A.D. 121. Emperor as 'Restorer of the World' (pp. 16, 77).

3. Aureus of Commodus, A.D. 192. Isis and Serapis (p. 17).

4. Cistophorous of Claudius I, A.D. 41-54. Diana Ephesia (p. 18).

5. Aureus of Julia Domna, *c*. A.D. 205. Cybele (pp. 17, 18).

6. Aureus of Septimius Severus, *c*. A.D. 204. Dea Caelestis (p. 18).

7. Aureus of Faustina I, *c*. A.D. 141. Consecration (Temple) (p. 27).

8. Aureus of Faustina I, *c*. A.D. 141. Consecration (Car in Procession to Circus) (p. 27).

9. Denarius of Tiberius, A.D. 14-37. The 'Tribute Penny' (pp. 9, 31).

10. Aureus of Nero, *c*. A.D. 65. Temple of Vesta (Reference to the Great Fire) (pp. 31,32).

11. Jewish Shekel of the First Revolt, A.D. 66-70 (p. 34).

12. Aureus of Domitian, A.D. 88. Herald of the Secular Games (p. 35).

13. Sestertius of Nerva, A.D. 97. 'Abuses of the Jewish Chest Removed' (pp. 34, 35).

14. Denarius of Trajan, *c*. A.D. 116. Roman 'Virtus' (p. 36).

PLATE I: INTRODUCTION — TRAJAN

PLATE II

1. Denarius of Hadrian, *c.* A.D. 127. Roman 'Virtus' (pp. 41, 42).

2. Jewish Shekel of the Second Revolt, *c.* A.D. 132-135 (p. 41).

3. Sestertius of Marcus Aurelius, A.D. 175. Temple of Thoth (the Egyptian Mercury) (p. 42).

4. Denarius of Commodus, A.D. 192. Club of Hercules (p. 42).

5. Aureus of Severus Alexander, *c.* A.D. 224. Jupiter the Preserver (p. 43).

6. Aureus of Julia Mammaea, *c.* A.D. 227. The Felicity of the State (p. 43).

7. Denarius of Maximin I, A.D. 235-238. Victory over Germany (p. 43).

8. Antoninianus of Philip I, A.D. 248. Secular Games (p. 43).

9. Antoninianus of Trajan Decius, A.D. 249-251. The Genius of the Army of Illyricum (p. 43).

10. Antoninianus of Divus Augustus, struck by Trajan Decius, A.D. 249-251 (p. 44).

11. Antoninianus of Valerian I, A.D. 254. Apollo the Preserver (p. 44).

12. Aureus of Gallienus, *c.* A.D. 267. 'Gallienae Augustae—Ubique Pax' (pp. 53, 54).

13. Antoninianus of Salonina, *c.* A.D. 264, struck at Milan. 'Augusta in Pace' (p. 54).

14. Antoninianus of Aurelian, *c.* A.D. 273. 'Restorer of the World' (p. 54).

15. As of Aurelian, A.D. 274. 'Sol Dominus Imperii Romani'— 'Aurelianus Augustus consecravit' (pp. 27, 54).

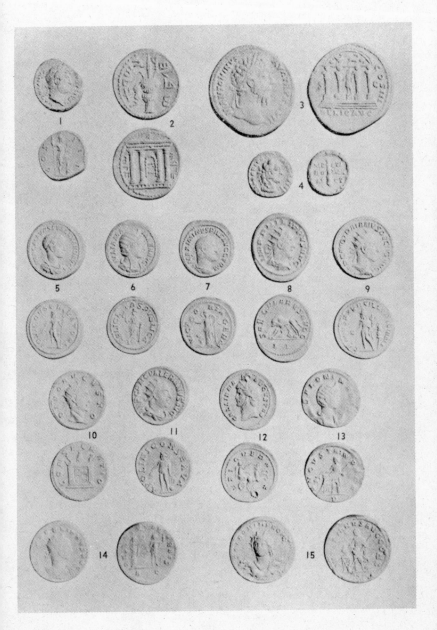

PLATE II: TRAJAN — AURELIAN

PLATE III

1. Aureus of Diocletian, c. A.D. 290. Jupiter the Preserver (pp. 27, 55, 56).

2. Aureus of Maximian, c. A.D. 300. Hercules and Hydra (p. 56).

3. Aureus of Galerius, c. A.D. 300. Mars the Champion (pp. 57, 58).

4. Bronze of Constantine the Great, c. A.D. 317. 'Soli Invicto Comiti'. Cross and star in field (pp. 59, 62).

5. Gold Medallion of Constantine, c. A.D. 330. Constantine II and Constantius II as Cæsars (pp. 62, 64, 65).

6. Bronze of Magnentius, c. A.D. 352-353. The Monogram of Christ, 'Alpha and Omega': 'The Salvation of our lords, the Augustus and Cæsar' (p. 67).

7. Bronze of Constans, c. A.D. 350. Emperor and Victory in a ship.

8. Bronze of Vetranio, A.D. 350. 'Hoc Signo Victor Eris' (the Vision of Constantine) (p. 67).

9. Bronze of Julian II, A.D. 362-363. 'The Security of the State': the bull Apis (pp. 67, 68).

10. Bronze of Valentinian I, c. A.D. 370. 'The Security of the State': Victory (p. 69).

11. Bronze of Theodosius I, c. A.D. 390. 'The Salvation of the State': Victory and captive (p. 70).

12. Bronze jeton, c. A.D. 400. 'Vota Publica': Isis and Serapis— Anubis.

13. Gold Medallion of Honorius. 'The Glory of the Romans' (p. 73).

PLATE III: DIOCLETIAN — HONORIUS

INDEX